Sacred and Desecrated:
Forty Days with Wendell Berry

Authors:

John Hewitt, Eli Jackson, Emily Mosher, Michelle Shackelford

ISBN: SBN-13: 978-1511840682
ISBN-10: 1511840684

Introduction:

This book is entitled *Sacred and Desecrated*, which is based on Wendell Berry's poem "How to Be a Poet." The poem includes the lines, "There are no unsacred places; there are only sacred places and desecrated places." The idea is that God has made all things holy because he is Holy. No matter what we do we cannot reduce their nature to 'unsacred' we can only desecrate them with our actions. For Berry this includes the land, animals, government, economy and our lives. In short, all creation is sacred, though some of it has been desecrated through the corruption of sin.

This book is to be used during Lent, the forty days that precede Easter. The purpose of Lent is to allow you to prepare your heart for the sorrow of Good Friday and the ecstatic Joy of Easter Sunday. This book includes a devotion for each day in Lent, with a focus on the care of creation. By creation we do not simply mean nature. Creation encompasses the entire cosmos, all that God has created; from forest trees to the inmost depth of the human soul. Wendell Berry has written much on creation and creation care, and so select quotations were selected to head each devotion.

The book is divided into six sections, each beginning with a challenge for the week, intended to provide ways to make what you are reading practical. Each day's devotion includes a quotation from Berry, a scripture verse or passage, followed by a short devotional reading. Also included are discussion questions that can be asked of a small group or reflected on individually, as well as a thematic prayer. As with all reading and devotional work, you will get out of it what you put into it.

The purpose of choosing the theme of creation care for this Lenten season is to remind us of the responsibility we have been given as stewards of this earth; and to remind us that how we treat God's creation affects how we treat each other and ourselves. We close this introduction with a poem that captures this idea beautifully.

Manifesto: The Mad Farmer Liberation Front

Love the quick profit, the annual raise,
vacation with pay. Want more
of everything ready-made. Be afraid
to know your neighbors and die.
And you will have a window in your head.
Not even your future will be a mystery
any more. Your mind will be a punched card
and shut away in a little drawer.
When they want you to buy something
they will call you. When they want you
to die for profit they will let you know.
So, friends, every day do something
that won't compute. Love the Lord.
Love the world. Work for nothing.
Take all that you have and be poor.
Love somebody who does not deserve it.
Denounce the government and embrace
the flag. Hope to live in that free
republic for which it stands.
Give your approval to all you cannot
understand. Praise ignorance, for what man
has not encountered he has not destroyed.
Ask the questions that have no answers.
Invest in the millennium. Plant sequoias.
Say that your main crop is the forest
that you did not plant,
that you will not live to harvest.
Say that the leaves are harvested
when they have rotted into the mold.
Call that profit. Prophesy such returns.
Put your faith in the two inches of humus
that will build under the trees
every thousand years.
Listen to carrion – put your ear

close, and hear the faint chattering
of the songs that are to come.
Expect the end of the world. Laugh.
Laughter is immeasurable. Be joyful
though you have considered all the facts.
So long as women do not go cheap
for power, please women more than men.
Ask yourself: Will this satisfy
a woman satisfied to bear a child?
Will this disturb the sleep
of a woman near to giving birth?
Go with you love to the fields.
Lie easy in the shade. Rest you head
in her lap. Swear allegiance
to what is nighest your thoughts.
As soon as the generals and the politicos
can predict the motions of your mind,
lost it. Leave it as a sign
to mark the false trail, the way
you didn't go. Be like the fox
who makes more tracks than necessary,
some in the wrong direction.
Practice resurrection.

New Collected Poems, "Manifesto: The Mad Farmer
Liberation Front," 173-174.

Community

CHALLENGE:

Make a list of three people in your life with whom you would like to have a more meaningful relationship with. Pray for them this week and make an effort to contact them. Eliminate small distractions in your life that prevent you from knowing and being known by others.

DAY ONE: DIMENSIONAL LIVING

"Live a three dimensioned life…"
New Collected Poems, "How to be a Poet," 354.

As iron sharpens iron, so one person sharpens another.
-Proverbs 27:17 NIV-

In a culture that is becoming more and more reliant on media and technology our relationships with other people often suffer. Many people are beginning to prefer engaging with others through social media and online communication, replacing face-to-face for face-to-screen communication. However, living life in "two dimensions" prevents us from experiencing true, biblical community.

Too often we allow the comfort of surface level relationships to create in us a stagnancy that permeates into other areas of our lives. If we are not careful we can begin to let how we interact with others relationally affect how we relate to God. God does not desire a surface level relationship with His children; He wants us to know and be known by Him. We should seek to have this approach in our relationships with others as well.

However, to know and be known by others requires a sense of vulnerability, something that can often be difficult for people. The fact of the matter is that experiencing meaningful community is not always easy and comfortable. The image of iron sharpening iron found in Proverbs 27:17 gives insight into what it looks like to experience meaningful fellowship with one another.

The act of smashing iron against iron is without a doubt beneficial for both blades as each are sharpened from contact, but what we often fail to see in this image is that the act is certainly not pretty. When two iron blades are struck together to be sharpened, sparks fly violently, but both products come out more refined. This is also true in our fellowship with one another. Human relationships aren't always perfect. In fact they are often difficult and challenging, but they are always worth it. Through these meaningful relationships we are shaped and refined.

Wendell Berry encourages others to "live a three dimensioned life", to be fully present in all areas of life. This is not only in regards to our relationship with God, but it also includes how we relate to humans, the land, and the rest of God's creation. Do you feel like you are experiencing meaningful relationships today? Pray that God will help you "live a three dimensioned life" and be fully present in your relationships.

Discussion Questions:

- ❖ What factors are preventing you from knowing and being known by others?
- ❖ How do we see our human relationships affecting our relationship with God?
- ❖ What can you do in your life in order to start living in "three dimensions"?

Prayer:

Lord you call us to be fully present in this life, to seek meaningful relationships with others as we continue to grow in You. We ask that You fill us with Your Spirit as we are transformed into the image of Christ. Cause the love of Christ to flow through us as we sharpen and are sharpened by others. Amen.

DAY TWO: SHARING WORDS

"Speaker and hearer, words making a passage between them, begin a community."

New Collected Poems, "The Handing Down," 41.

Death and life are in the power of the tongue, and those who love it will eat its fruits.

-Proverbs 18:21 NRSV-

I learned in my undergraduate speech class that communication is the sharing of an idea between two people, the sender and the receiver. To express verbal communication, my professor drew a picture of two people and sound waves between them. To my eye, the sound waves looked like a bridge that closed the gap between two individuals who otherwise may not know one another.

A quick dictionary.com search reveals that the origin of the word "communication" comes from the word "common," from which also originates the word "community." To be in community means at least to hold something in common, and the sharing of those common things often comes in communication of some sort.

Listening is one of the greatest gifts we can give someone. To allow another person to know that we will give our full attention to him or her for however long a time is necessary can be incredibly healing.

Sharing our own stories is also a wonderful gift. To hold shared experience in common is to lay the foundation for true, deep community. Even among friends who grow up in very different parts of the world or who have had very different life experiences, sharing those experiences builds bridges that lead to lasting, healing relationships.

True community can be hard to find, and it takes time to build. Perhaps the beginning of community is building bridges between people. Perhaps we begin to find our common ground and enter into a place of safe trust with others when we communicate our stories and share our experiences, as both speaker and listener.

Discussion:
- ❖ Can you describe a time when you have felt embraced by community? How did that serve to shape and change you?
- ❖ If community begins by building bridges, how do we work to maintain those bridges over time?

Prayer:
Loving God, thank you for the gift of community, where we can be truly embraced in the arms of love just as we are. Remind me today of those around me who have been those loving arms. Open my eyes to the possibilities of new friends whom I can embrace. Amen.

DAY THREE: COMMUNITY AND COMPETITION

"But what the ideal of competition most flagrantly and disastrously excludes is affection....For human beings, affection is the ultimate motive, because the force that powers us, as Ruskin also said, is not 'steam, magnetism, or gravitation,' but 'a Soul.'"
  The Art of the Commonplace, "Economy & Pleasure," 212.

For it was you who formed my inward parts; you knit me together in my mother's womb. I praise you, for I am fearfully and wonderfully made. Wonderful are your works; that I know very well.

-Psalm 139:13-14 NRSV-

Any good business person knows that in order to stay in business, one must know how to compete. Competition is the way of survival in today's world. We see it when a locally owned restaurant is pushed to closure after the chain restaurants come to town. We see it when local grocery stores go bankrupt because they cannot keep their prices lower than Wal-Mart. We see it when small-business gift shops shut their doors because consumers prefer the brands they find at corporate stores. If a business is unable to compete, it loses and is knocked out of the race.

What about on the personal level? As members of society, do we sometimes begin to compete with one another for the best things? Perhaps we look out the window at our neighbors who have a new car and think, "I would like to have one of those." Maybe we see a friend who has a nice new outfit and tell ourselves, "You don't have anything that nice in your closet." Or perhaps when we see one of our friends surrounded by a group of people we do not know, we feel left out and think that they live more fun lives than we do. We have all done it.

When those thoughts come to our minds, how do we respond? Sometimes when I see something nice that someone else has, I feel the urge to go out and buy something like it. Then when I get home, I feel empty inside rather than being personally fulfilled.

Berry notes that when we are driven by competition, we are excluding affection, the thing our souls most need and the thing that makes us human. When we live by competition, instead of looking at another person and seeing him or her as human, we look at his or her possessions and see only what is on the outside.

Have you ever been in relationship with someone who could see right through all the fronts you put up? No matter how hard you try to put up pretenses that make your life look like the person you wish you could be, that person sees straight through to who you truly are. Those friendships are an incredible gift, for they enable us to share deep community and affection. When we can freely express our deepest selves to another person, it opens us to receive the deepest gift we could ever receive – love.

The psalmist reminds us that we have been crafted intricately, all the tiny pieces of our souls woven in the depths of our mothers' wombs. When we share those intricacies in relationship with others, rather than living in competition with them, we have a new reason to praise God, because we are reminded that God's works truly are wonderful.

Discussion:
- ❖ Have you ever found yourself comparing your life or possessions to others'? How did that leave you feeling?
- ❖ What would it look like to begin sharing your true self deeply in a trusting relationship with someone in your life? Would you be open to the affection you might find there?

Prayer:
God, thank you that you are so creative that you can craft all the creatures in the world individually, differently, and wonderfully. Thank you for the gifts you have given to me. Help me to realize my unique place in the world and to love others in theirs, rather than comparing. Amen.

DAY FOUR: LEARING TO FORGIVE

"If God loves the ones we can't...then finally maybe we can."
That Distant Land, "Pray Without Ceasing", 70.

Bear with each other and forgive one another if any of you has a grievance against someone. Forgive as the Lord forgave you.
-Colossians 3:13-

Forgiveness tends to be one of the hardest things for Christians to implement into their lives. We are wronged by people every day, but often we find ourselves unwilling to forgive certain individuals for how they have hurt us personally or through someone we love. Our unwillingness to forgive leads to separation, which leads to estrangement, which ultimately leads to a total lack of love. We become calloused and resistant to reconciliation.

But how does this measure up to what we believe about God? We often say that God in His very being is the prime example of grace and forgiveness. His love goes beyond the weight of human sin and looks past our wrongdoings, leading us not into estrangement, but reconciliation. Along with this belief about God's character we trust that, through the work of the Holy Spirit, we are being transformed into the image of Christ. Thus we conclude that as we are following Christ we are becoming more and more like him.

So the real question is, if we are not willing to forgive others, are we also not willing to accept God's forgiveness in our own lives? We are called as Christians to imitate Christ not only in the easy things, but also in the hard moments such as forgiving others for wronging us. Think of it this way, has there ever been a moment in your life where you longed for someone to forgive you? Have you ever felt the weight and conviction of your wrongdoing and desired for forgiveness, even it might not have been deserved? How much did your heart yearn for reconciliation? As followers of Christ we should feel this same desire when others have wronged us.

Wendell Berry sees that this type of forgiveness and love for others is difficult. In his short story "Pray Without Ceasing", a family is dealing with the murder of one of their own by a man in the community. Even though they dealt with real anger and disbelief, they began to take a step back and realize the power of God's forgiveness. One of the characters states, "If God love the ones we can't...then finally maybe we can."

C.S. Lewis states that we can implement forgiveness in our lives by "meaning our words when we say in our prayers each night 'Forgive our trespasses as we forgive those that trespass against us...'" If we gladly accept the forgiveness of God we must also implement the same forgiveness in our daily relationships.

Discussion Questions:
- ❖ What usually prevents you from forgiving someone?
- ❖ Have you ever wronged someone and sincerely desired his or her forgiveness? How did that make you feel?
- ❖ Read Colossians 3:13, how can you apply this verse actively in your life today?

Prayer:
Heavenly Father, you are the ultimate example of forgiveness. We thank You for Your Son, who came to earth and wronged no one, but died for our sins all the same. Give us Your heart of forgiveness today. Amen.

DAY FIVE: TRANSFORMING SELFISHNESS TO SELFLESSNESS

"From the union of self-gratification and self-annihilation
secede into care for one another
and for the good gifts of Heaven and Earth."
New Collected Poems, "The Mad Farmer, Flying the Flag of Rough
Branch, Secedes from the Union," 327.

Then he said to them all, "If any want to become my followers, let them deny themselves and take up their cross daily and follow me. For those who want to save their life will lose it, and those who lose their life for my sake will save it. What does it profit them if they gain the whole world, but lose or forfeit themselves? Those who are ashamed of me and of my words, of them the Son of Man will be ashamed when he comes in his glory and the glory of the Father and of the holy angels. But truly I tell you, there are some standing here who will not taste death before they see the kingdom of God."

-Luke 9:23-27 NRSV-

Jesus' words rarely are easy to hear and obey. When we read the gospels, we are constantly challenged to choose a path that looks different from what the world would have us do. Following Jesus is hard, and it demands our full dedication. Though our American culture may value success, money, and power, Jesus teaches us to choose love, to care for one another even when that involves sacrifice, just as he did. Berry's poem challenges us to take Jesus' words seriously and think about how our desires to fulfill all of our wants can actually lead to self-destruction. Instead, he asks us to focus on caring for one another, which will improve not only our community but also our own lives as well.

Discussion Questions:

 ❖ Think of a difficult time when you had to choose whether or not to place someone else's needs above your own. What factors did you consider when making your decision?
 ❖ What were the results? Would you choose differently now?
 ❖ What do you think are "the good gifts of Heaven and Earth" that Berry is referring to?

Prayer:

Lord, we know that following you is not an easy task. Please give us the strength we need to continue in your footsteps. Help us to recognize the things we want that our selfish or hurtful, and instead fill us with your love so that we will desire to share it. Amen.

DAY SIX: A COMMUNITY OF HEALING

"I turn against you, I break from you, I turn to you. We hurt, and are hurt, and have each other for healing..."
New Collected Poems, "Marriage", 81.

Therefore confess your sins to each other and pray for each other so that you may be healed. The prayer of a righteous person is powerful and effective.

-James 5:16 NIV-

In our daily lives we are often faced with various trials and hurts. It is part of being human. It is often in these times that the last thing we want to do is be around other people. We seek healing from other facets of life: television, food, mindlessly surfing the internet, etc. However, these things often fill us for a moment but leave us empty again. In these moments one must realize the importance of community as God's gift to us for growth and healing.

The original audience of the book of James is an example of a people hurting and facing many trials. They were Jews who had recently accepted the Christian faith as their own but found themselves under persecution after the stoning of Stephen (Acts 7). They had been stripped of their land and homes in Jerusalem and forced to form smaller communities throughout the region. Not only were they facing trials from those outside of their community, but also from within as they wrestled with their current situation and how it related to their newfound faith.

It is during this time of suffering that James steps in as a pastoral figure, encouraging the people to remain faithful even though they were experiencing hardships. James points to the community of believers that his audience was connected to as a means of healing. In James 5:16 they are encouraged to rely on each other during such a time of pain, to confess their sins and pray for one another while seeking healing. It is in these moments when the Body of Christ gathers together that God's presence is truly made known and healing can occur.

Wendell Berry describes this type of healing beautifully when writing about his wife: "We hurt, and are hurt, and have each other for healing." Even in times of pain and sorrow God gives us the gift of community to help comfort and renew us. We must never underestimate the healing power of Christian love and community.

Discussion Questions:

- ❖ What things do you find yourself running to besides God and others for healing?
- ❖ What are some ways you can seek meaningful relationships in your life?
- ❖ How does the context of James and his audience's situation change your understanding of James 5:16?

Prayer:

God, we acknowledge You as creator, sustainer, and comforter. Help us love and comfort others as we come together in community and honor Your Son as healer and savior. Amen.

DAY SEVEN: THE WEDDING OF LOVE AND SUFFERING

"To love is to suffer—did I
know this when first
I asked you for your love?
I did not. And yet until
I knew, I could not know what
I asked, or gave. I gave
a suffering that I took: yours
and mine, mine when yours;
and yours I have feared the most."
New Collected Poems, "Duality, I" 328.

But if you marry, you do not sin, and if a virgin marries, she does not sin. Yet those who marry will experience distress in this life, and I would spare you that... I want you to be free from anxieties. The unmarried man is anxious about the affairs of the Lord, how to please the Lord; but the married man is anxious about the affairs of the world, how to please his wife, and his interests are divided. And the unmarried woman and the virgin are anxious about the affairs of the Lord, so that they may be holy in body and spirit; but the married woman is anxious about the affairs of the world, how to please her husband. I say this for your own benefit, not to put any restraint upon you, but to promote good order and unhindered devotion to the Lord.

-1 Corinthians 7:28, 32-35 NRSV-

The passage above was shared with me by a missionary while I was working in Tanzania for a semester. I was young and single. The missionary told me that it was a blessing that I was single for this stage, because I could focus more keenly on God. Being young and single, I did not view this as such a blessing, but since then I have learned the truth of her, and Paul's words.

Paul is certainly not commanding anyone that they must remain single. This is one of the few instances where he explicitly tells us that this is his opinion (v. 25). Yet, Paul does realize that marriage entails the entangling process of two lives, which creates unity, but entails some suffering. Marriage is a process of dying to oneself, and can beautifully reflect a Christian life. Both instances involve love and suffering. Any union that does not involve this is founded on self-service and selfish actions.

Wendell Berry has seized the truth of this poignantly when he says, "to love is to suffer." Each of us bring anxiety to the table, when these anxieties come together after the emotion expression of love has faded, it can only result in conflict. However, there is something profoundly moving about a couple who have remained faithful to each other through the years. As you look at the way they look at each other, you can see the pain shared and the beauty created.

The essence of what both Paul and Berry are getting at is that love in our fallen world involves suffering, and to enter into marriage is a profound commitment. Marriage is not to be taken lightly.

Discussion Questions:

No matter whether you are married or single the message of Paul and Wendell Berry can have implications for you, since all relationships involve love, trust and the possibility for suffering.

- ❖ How does our culture's view of marriage/relationships differ from the one above?
- ❖ How does this profoundly different view of relationships affect the longevity and depth of a marriage or relationship?
- ❖ Think about the relationships you are and have been in. Do you actions resemble self-sacrifice or self-service? How can you take steps to improve this?

Prayer:

> We pray, oh God, that our relationships can more closely match your love for us, then our love for you. Let our actions demonstrate love, not self-love. Let us again take our relationships seriously, because you do. Meet our unlove with your love, so we can love those around us, even in suffering.
>
> Glory be to the Father, and to the Son, and to the Holy Spirit.
> As it was in the beginning, is now and ever shall ever be, world without end.
> Alleluia.
> Amen.

Embodied Faith and Daily Living

CHALLENGE:

As you reflect on these devotions concerning everyday living, begin to make a list of 3 areas in your life that you wish to work on. Having trouble forgiving someone? Struggling to find times of silence with God? Put together this list and begin to implement these practices in your daily life.

DAY EIGHT: REMEMBERING TO REMEMBER

"We owe the future the past, the long knowledge that is the potency of time to come."

New Collected Poems, "At a Country Funeral," 184.

Is this the way you repay the LORD, O foolish and unwise people? Is he not your Father, your Creator, who made you and formed you? Remember the days of old; consider the generations long past. Ask your father and he will tell you, your elders, and they will explain to you.

-Deuteronomy 32:6-7-

We live in a time where the majority of people focus their gaze towards the future. Time spent in the present is predominately used to prepare, plan, and see our future play out into fruition. We study diligently for a college degree to ensure a good job down the road, we have a retirement plan to secure the hope of future relaxation, and we save up "rainy day" funds to combat the unexpected future. These things are not bad, in fact most of them are quite important and helpful. However, one thing is certain: we tend to place the future at the highest point of priority.

It doesn't take much to realize the human desire of reaching the "future self." For instance, one can hardly walk around a new or used bookstore and not be bombarded by thousands of self-help books. These books are usually titled with a specific numerical step program and a tag of how we can plan for the future or ensure success down the road. It is painfully obvious where our minds are focused on.

In fact, we are often led to believe that the past is something that we should avoid. We are told that living in the past holds us back from our future and is ultimately unhealthy. This is particularly true in the life of Christians. We view the past as something that we can let go of and forget because of God's forgiveness and His desire to move us forward. While it is true that we are fully forgiven and freed from the mistakes of the past, it is doing the future a disservice to completely discard the past.

The people of Israel are an excellent example of the dangers of forgetting the past. God's people underwent years of slavery by the hands of the Egyptians, but the Lord heard their cries and delivered them from their bondage through his servant Moses.

The Israelites were constantly reminded of God's faithfulness and saw firsthand His power and provision. However, as time went on they forgot the amazing things God had done for them, enabling them to slip into idolatry and sin. Moses' desire for the people to remember what God had done for them shows how the importance of the past: "Remember the days of old; consider the generations long past."

The past can be a very important tool to inform our present and future. Through retrospect we can view clearly God's faithfulness and provision in our life. Wendell Berry puts it well when he states that "we owe the future the past." By remembering how God brought us through a hard time, how we received spiritual healing, or a time when the Lord provided an answered prayer we allow our past to serve the future in a purposeful way.

Discussion Questions:

❖ Do you tend to focus on the future too often? What are the things you worry about when thinking about the future?
❖ Why do you think we often forget about what God has done for us in the past? How do we combat this forgetfulness?
❖ Can you think of a time where God was faithful in a chaotic moment in your life?

Prayer:

Heavenly Father, we ask that you make Yourself known to us in our lives today. Help us to remember Your faithfulness as we look forward to what you have planned for us in the future. Amen.

DAY NINE: A RECONCILING LOVE

"I take literally the statement in the Gospel of John that God loves the world. I believe that the world was created and approved by love, that it subsists, coheres, and endures by love, and that, insofar as it is redeemable, it can be redeemed only by love. I believe that divine love, incarnate and indwelling in the world, summons the world always toward wholeness, which ultimately is reconciliation and atonement with God."

The Art of the Commonplace, "Health Is Membership," 146.

For God so loved the world...

-John 3:16-

And now these three remain: faith, hope and love. But the greatest of these is love.

-1 Corinthians 13:13-

The love of God is one of the most talked about topics within the Christian faith. We talk about His love healing us, forgiving us, and ultimately bringing us into reconciliation with Him. In fact, one could say that God's love is the overarching theme of Scripture. However, the Enlightenment and the hyper-individualism that came with the movement has shifted a holistic view of God's love into merely something between an individual and his Creator. What we have lost from this type of thinking is the fact that God's love does not only reconcile the individual but brings reconciliation to the whole of creation.

God's love was truly made manifest by his Son Jesus Christ who made the ultimate sacrifice even though our sin continued to run rampant. Through Jesus Christ we have received salvation and have been completely redeemed and able to have fellowship with God. As redeemed people our lives should reflect God's love to everyone and everything that surrounds us. Too often the Christian faith in America has become focused on the individual. We ask questions like, 'How can **I** experience God's love more fully?', or, 'How do I know that God is working through **me**?' However, God's love encompasses far beyond the individual Christian and reaches the full scope of the created order. As ambassadors of Christ, our lives should mirror a holistic view of God's love.

For instance, in light of God's love for the world, Christians must seek the welfare and reconciliation of God's creation. This includes fighting for justice around the world, sharing the love of Christ globally, and being good stewards of what God has given to us. God's love is not only something that he gives to us, but it is something that he commands us to give and show to others. In a world that puts so many other things at the forefront we are called to champion love as the greatest quality.

Through God's love for us we are enabled to not only fully love others, but also come alongside God in bringing wholeness to the world. Berry rightly states that the world "can be redeemed only by love", and through that love we bring people into reconciliation with God. Let the love of God endure in your life today.

Discussion Questions:

- ❖ What ways have you experienced God's love in your own life? How can you use this experience to spread the love of God to others?
- ❖ What do you think it means to 'reconcile' creation through the love of God? Can you think of any concrete examples?
- ❖ Read 1 Corinthians 3:13 again. How does Paul's teachings on love compare to Jesus' "Greatest Commandment"

Prayer:

God we thank you for Your love and how it brings reconciliation to Your people. Help us use that love for the sake of others, to come alongside You in bringing reconciliation to the word. Amen.

DAY TEN: THE COURAGE OF FAITHFULNESS

"The drama of ordinary or daily behavior also raises the issue of courage, but it raises at the same time the issue of skill; and, because ordinary behavior lasts so much longer than heroic action, it raises in a more complex and difficult way the issue of perseverance. It may, in some way, be easier to be Samson than to be a good husband or wife day after day for fifty years."

The Art of the Commonplace, "The Gift of Good Land," 300.

So let us not grow weary in doing what is right, for we will reap at harvest-time, if we do not give up. So then, whenever we have an opportunity, let us work for the good of all, and especially for those of the family of faith.

-Galatians 6:9-10 NRSV-

If someone asked you to name a biblical character or story you admired, who would it be? You might think of Noah, who built the arc while others mocked him. You might name Moses, who parted the waters to lead the Israelites out of Egypt. Maybe you would consider Samson, whose great strength brought down a house to kill thousands of Philistines. Perhaps you would look to Peter, Paul, or other apostles who bravely shared the gospel and taught countless people about Christ.

How many people would think of Shiphrah and Puah, the midwives who day after day prevented Hebrew babies from being turned over to the Pharaoh to be murdered? Who would think of Ruth and her decision to remain with her mother-in-law even though it meant learning to live in a foreign country? Would you think of the thousands of nameless people baptized by the apostles who devoted their lives to following Christ in ordinary ways (Acts 2:41-42)?

It's easy to get discouraged when we compare ourselves to our heroes and think that our faith isn't strong enough or that we aren't making enough of a difference in the world, but the Bible is full of stories of ordinary people living ordinary lives to the glory of God even in the midst of the extraordinary acts of God. We occasionally may be a part of these extraordinary events, but most days we wake up and go to work and take care of our loved ones. If done well, however, these small acts are just as heroic and require even more perseverance and faithfulness.

A strong marriage isn't built on one fantastic memory, but on the dedication and love that is exhibited day after day. The same is true of any relationship, whether that be with a family member, a friend, or even God.

Discussion Questions:

❖ Can you name another biblical story that is often overlooked but demonstrates "ordinary" faithfulness?
❖ What is one ordinary thing that you struggle to do well every day? What effect does it have on your life and others' lives?
❖ What could you do to improve in that one area?

Prayer:

Lord, we thank you for these stories that have been passed down to us of courageous men and women who were obedient to you day after day, year after year. Their stories remind us that even when we think we can't feel your presence, you are present with us through your Holy Spirit, who continues to guide and strengthen us. Whether we are weary or joyful when we start our day, help us to be faithful. Amen.

DAY ELEVEN: A TRANSFORMATIONAL JOURNEY

"I think the issues of 'identity' mostly
are poppycock. We are what we have done,
which includes our promises, includes
our hopes, but promises first."
            -*New Collected Poems*, "Some Further Words," 360.

Read 2 Kings 2:1-12 (A portion is included below)
When they had crossed, Elijah said to Elisha, "Tell me what I may do for you, before I am taken from you." Elisha said, "Please let me inherit a double share of your spirit." He responded, "You have asked a hard thing; yet, if you see me as I am being taken from you, it will be granted you; if not, it will not." As they continued walking and talking, a chariot of fire and horses of fire separated the two of them, and Elijah ascended in a whirlwind into heaven. Elisha kept watching and crying out, "Father, father! The chariots of Israel and its horsemen!" But when he could no longer see him, he grasped his own clothes and tore them in two pieces.
                                        -2 Kings 2:9-12 NRSV-

        This narrative records the final act of Elijah's grand play, and the transition from him to his protégé Elisha. In the passage Elijah takes Elisha on a meandering journey through Israel's history making stops at Gilgal (the first campsite in the promised land after miraculously crossing the Jordan under the leadership of Joshua); Bethel (where Abram built an altar and Jacob saw a ladder to heaven, as well as a resting place for the tabernacle); Jericho (the site of Israel's first great victory in the land); the Jordan (where Joshua's leadership is confirmed with a miraculous parting and crossing on dry land); and finally the wilderness beyond the Jordan (where God sustained the people of Israel for forty years).

Three times during this journey Elijah approaches Elisha and tells him to stop, and remain where they are. Each time is in a city of profound religious significance. All three times Elisha refuses to the point of taking an oath to follow his mentor to the end. In addition to this, he is twice approached by a company of prophets telling him that his master will be taken from him. Each time he affirms their observation, silences them and follows his master.

Finally, after leaving a crowd and Israel behind, they cross the Jordan in a way similar to Joshua, and Elijah turns to share last words with his student. Elisha is given a last request, and he boldly asks for a double portion of the spirit of Elijah.

According to Deuteronomy 21:17, a double portion was to be given to the firstborn son indicating him as the true heir of the father. Elijah reminds him that to be his true heir will be no walk in the park. His ministry has included a divine showdown and encounters with God, but it also included despair, a murderous king and queen, and deep suffering. But Elijah grants him this request on the condition that he witness Elijah's ascension into heaven.

What follows is an extraordinary event in which Elisha is separated from his master by a fiery chariot, who is taken into heaven by a rushing whirlwind. Elisha is left alone with the pain of loss and tears his clothes in mourning. But where is his double portion? Where is his initiation ceremony? How exactly is he supposed to receive his inheritance?

It is here that we realize that no miraculous event imparts the character of a prophet. It is the journey that is transformative. It was Elisha's faithfulness to his master, and his word, refusing to accept his office prematurely when it is offered by the prophets. Wendell Berry reminds us that our identity includes our hopes and our promises. It is the promises kept, and the little actions on the road of life that transform us. If we are still waiting for a ceremony that makes us like Christ, we have missed the point and have stopped short.

Discussion Questions:

Elisha refused to take shortcuts, and refused to break his word. It was in these actions that he was transformed in the heir of Elijah.

- ❖ How often do you truly keep your word? How often do you break it?
- ❖ How do the little, daily actions add up to transform a person's character?
- ❖ What shortcuts and half-truths have affected your life? What can you do to change this?

Prayer:

We pray, oh God, that our word can reflect your Word. Your Word took on flesh for the redemption of us all. We pray that we can be honest with ourselves and others. We pray that we can refuse shortcuts and half-measures. We pray that our daily actions add up to a life that demonstrates your love.

Glory be to the Father, and to the Son, and to the Holy Spirit.
As it was in the beginning, is now and ever shall ever be, world without end.
Alleluia.
Amen.

DAY TWELVE: THE VOICE IN THE SILENCE

"Accept what comes from silence. Make the best you can of it. Of the little words that come out of the silence, like prayers prayed back to the one who prays, make a poem that does not disturb the silence from which it came."

New Collected Poems, "How to be a Poet" 354.

Yes, my soul, find rest in God; my hope comes from him.

-Psalm 62:5 NIV-

Silence can often be terrifying. This is mainly due the fact that we tend to glorify the hustle and bustle of busyness, never leaving ourselves opportunities to quiet ourselves. In fact we attach negative connotations to the word silence as we call it "awkward" and even "deafening". However, these terms merely reflect a skewed view of silence, considering that quieting ourselves and getting away from the busyness of life often leads to meaningful reflection. Canceling out the noises of life helps us center ourselves towards renewal, and allows us to be aware of God's voice. We see solitude and silence exemplified through the life of Jesus as he constantly saw the need to get away and spend time alone with God.

So what keeps us from experiencing the beauty of silence in our lives? One particular reason is the fact that silence often leaves us uncomfortable. We often get into the habit of thinking that we always have to be doing something in order to find meaning in life. We believe the lie that we can only be formed spiritually if we are constantly active in our pursuit of Christ. However, often the best thing for a believer who desires to be formed spiritually is to disengage from the responsibilities of life in order to reconnect with God. Silence brings back to alignment with the Lord as we come to Him bearing a clean slate, not the baggage of pressing responsibilities and concerns. It is in these moments that God speaks to us the most and we can hear His voice most clearly.

Wendell Berry acknowledges the importance of silence in his own life, stating that one should "accept what comes from silence." Often we avoid silence became we are not willing to accept what comes from it. We know that during those moments of silence God might call us to do something we are unwilling to do. This could be forgiving someone who has hurt us, adjusting our finances to include caring for the poor, or simply God exposing a sin in our lives. However, it is only in these moments of silence that we can begin to respond to God's desires for our lives. Although it is sometimes uncomfortable, silence leads us to an intimacy with God and in turn creates in us a deeper desire for holiness. Allow yourself to find time for silence in your life today. Find rest in God through His ever-present love.

Discussion Questions:

- ❖ Do you find time for silence with God in your life? If not, what is preventing you from participating in moments of silence?
- ❖ In what ways has silence been uncomfortable for you?
- ❖ Can you think of a place where you can practice silence in your life today?

Prayer:

God, create in us a desire for silence as we seek to hear Your voice. In the busyness of life and the concerns that come from it help us rest in the knowledge that You are faithful and that we can place our hope in You, Amen.

DAY THIRTEEN: LIVING YOUR PART

"No matter how much one may love the world as a whole, one can live fully in it only by living responsibly in some small part of it."
The Art of the Commonplace, "The Body and the Earth," 118.

For it will be like a man going on a journey, who called his servants and entrusted to them his property. To one he gave five talents, to another two, to another one, to each according to his ability. Then he went away. He who had received the five talents went at once and traded with them, and he made five talents more. So also he who had the two talents made two talents more. But he who had received the one talent went and dug in the ground and hid his master's money. Now after a long time the master of those servants came and settled accounts with them. And he who had received the five talents came forward, bringing five talents more, saying, "Master, you delivered to me five talents; here I have made five talents more." His master said to him, "Well done, good and faithful servant. You have been faithful over a little; I will set you over much. Enter into the joy of your master."

-Matthew 25:14-21 NRSV-

Poor nutrition causes 45% of deaths in children under five – that's 3.1 million children each year. In Sub-Saharan Africa, one in four people are undernourished. In the United States, nearly 50% of public school students are eligible for free or reduced-price lunch because their families cannot afford to provide them with nutritious meals every day. Many of these children will not have three meals a day during the summer.[1]

---

[1] Statistics from http://www.wfp.org/hunger/stats and https://nces.ed.gov/programs/digest/d13/tables/dt13_204.10.asp.

Depressing statistics can leave us feeling overwhelmed by big issues like world hunger, health care, or human rights. We may get discouraged and think that either we don't know enough about the issue to solve the problem or that our contribution would be too small to matter. Berry encourages us to look not at global issues throughout the world, but to get to know our own community, the people who live in it, and the challenges they face. Each of us has skills and interests we can use to make our community a better place for everyone who calls it home. If we work together and are faithful with what God gives us, no matter where we live or what our occupations are, then we will make a difference that matters to our neighbors.

Questions:
- ❖ What are some challenges currently facing people in your community?
- ❖ What is one issue in your community you would like to learn more about, and what skills might you be able to contribute to help improve it?
- ❖ Who do you know who would like to join you in this effort?

Prayer:
God, we know that you made us in your image, which means that we also have the potential for a creativity that can bring life to deserted places. We also know that made each of us with different talents, interests, and gifts from the Holy Spirit so that we can serve you. Teach us to be faithful with what you have given us and to bravely go forward into our communities to join you in the work of redemption and reconciliation that you have already started. Amen.

DAY FOURTEEN: A LIFETIME OF DAYS

"When I rise up
let me rise up joyful
like a bird.

When I fall
let me fall without regret
like a leaf."

New Collected Poems, "Prayers and Sayings of the Mad
Farmer." *149.*

*Then he said to them all, "If any want to become my followers, let
them deny themselves and take up their cross daily and follow me.
For those who want to save their life will lose it, and those who
lose their life for my sake will save it. What does it profit them if
they gain the whole world, but lose or forfeit themselves?"*
-Luke 9:23-25 NRSV-

Life is a series of cycles. The seasons rotate through their
appointed times, and the sun and moon take turns keeping vigil
over the world. The poetic expression of creation in Genesis one
describes God creating in days beginning and ending with evening
and morning; each day bringing something new to the created
order.

Likewise, our lives are governed by and composed of days.
Each evening we witness the consistency of the cycles as the sun
sets, and when the weather is just right it disappears in a riot of
colors that have captivate the artist and unartistic alike. Each
morning the sun peeks over the horizon casting rays of light about
announcing the time for life to blossom. No matter who we are a
day is a day, and cannot be governed by our actions. However, what
we choose to do with the day is another matter.

The passage above follows Peter's confession of Jesus' role as Messiah and Son of God, which is followed by Jesus reframing the idea of Messiah as someone who has to suffer. In this verse Jesus warns his followers that suffering is part of Christian discipleship, through the use of the metaphor of "carrying one's cross. Luke's version of this account includes the critical word "daily." It is not enough for a person to give her all to Christ and then live like she did not. Even discipleship is governed by the cycle of life. Daily we must take up our cross to follow our Lord. It is an intentional action of dying to self.

Wendell Berry recognizes this cyclical pattern in life. His quotation above could equally be applied to both life, and a day. If we end each day without regret then we will live a life without regret. I love his imagery of a leaf falling without regret. The leaf has budded spread itself out to collect the energy and when its time is done it does the only sensible thing, die. This death is not a giving up, or capitulation. It is simply the recognition that it is not the tree. The life of the leaf has added to the overall health of the tree and when its cycle is complete it falls without regret and provides additional nutrients to the soil for the continual use by the tree.

Likewise, we need to recognize that we are not the whole of world, humanity, or even the church. We are like the leaf who can add to the health of the world, but we are more than a leaf and can also do immeasurable damage to the world's health. As we travel the cycles of life, it is helpful to continue to ask ourselves, "Are the achievements of this day aligned with my hearts deepest yearning for grace-filled living?"[2] Daily live in such a way as to take up your cross and follow our savior, and perhaps in the giving up of your life, you may just save it.

---

[2] Macrina Wiederkehr, *Seven Sacred Pauses*, Sorin Books, Notre Dame: 2008, 155.

Discussion Questions:

- ❖ How do the choices of yesterday affect our choices today?
- ❖ What did Jesus mean by "take up your cross and follow me?"
- ❖ What would it look like if you lived each day without regrets, or at least a minimal amount? Would your life look different?
- ❖ What are some practical steps you could take to make this a reality?

Prayer:

We pray, oh God, that in the morning we rise up joyful like a bird, and when we fall, we fall without regret like a leaf. And a lifetime of these days can be well spent in service to your Kingdom, as we daily take up our cross and follow you.

Glory be to the Father, and to the Son, and to the Holy
	Spirit.
As it was in the beginning, is now and ever shall ever be,
	world without end.
Alleluia.
Amen

Land, Creation and Wilderness

CHALLENGE:

This week, go to a park or forest, or get out in the country, and look at the wildness of God's creation. While there, take a moment to silence your busy mind and heart. Then reflect on the danger and opportunity that comes with entering the wilderness. Remember the Israelites as they stood on the brink of the wilderness in which they would travel for a generation. Thank God for providing when we can't make it on our own.

DAY FIFTEEN: CREATION SPEAKS

"Where is our comfort but in the free, uninvolved, finally mysterious beauty and grace of this world that we did not make, that has no price? Where is our sanity but there? Where is our pleasure but in working and resting kindly in the presence of this world?"

The Art of the Commonplace, "Economy & Pleasure," 215.

The heavens are telling the glory of God; and the firmament proclaims his handiwork. Day to day pours forth speech, and night to night declares knowledge. There is no speech, nor are there words; their voice is not heard; yet their voice goes out through all the earth, and their words to the end of the world.

-Psalm 19:1-4 NRSV-

It was a time in which I could find no peace. The days were dark inside my soul, though outside the sun shone so brightly that it hurt my eyes. The brilliant sun in God's beautiful earth did not match the shade of night I carried inside.

On one of my worst days, I took a walk outside. I went down to the river, to a bridge where, if I looked off to one side, the water seemed to be coming at me, and if I looked off to the other side, the water was going away. The narrow river was surrounded on each side by trees whose branches hung over the water, providing shade for the waters near the bank. Though there was little peace to be found in my soul, my mind began to sing the words to the old hymn "It is Well with My Soul."

After I silently watched the water for quite some time, I saw a turtle near the bank come up above the water, then below, then back up again. I have long considered turtles a symbol of courage.

The most striking creature of all was a tiny little white fish. I am not sure how I noticed her (I decided she must have been a girl), because she was so small, but for several minutes, she captured my attention. The current was coming toward me, not swiftly but with enough speed to keep the water steadily moving. The little fish swam from one side of the river to the other, sometimes directly against the current and sometimes perpendicular to it. Once she got to the other side, she turned around and swam back to the side where she began.

I was so intrigued by this brave little fish! She could have swum easily down the river with the current, going wherever it took her but lacking no direction of her own. Instead, she knew where she wanted to be, and so she put forth the necessary effort to get there.

On a day when my soul could find no peace, I found great comfort in her courage and determination, and I gave thanks to God for a creation that speaks so clearly God's truth, without having ever said a word.

Discussion Questions:
- ❖ Can you think of a time when you found solace in creation? In what ways did that experience speak to you?
- ❖ Does it bring your mind peace to know that you did not create this world, and you cannot sustain it? Why or why not?

Prayer:
God of all Creation, thank you for the works of your hands that remind us who we are. Thank you for the healing that comes to us in all you have made. Help us to see more clearly the ways in which you reveal yourself this day. Amen.

DAY SIXTEEN: A HOLY VISION

"The world is a holy vision, had we clarity to see it."
New Collected Poems, "The Mad Farmer Manifesto: To the
First Amendment," 177.

God saw everything that he had made, and indeed, it was very good. And there was evening and there was morning, the sixth day.

-Genesis 1:31 NRS-

So often we operate in this world as if it did not exist. The only thing that exists is the next assignment, appointment, meeting, sale, or even day. It is so easy to forget to look up. It often takes a poet to remind us that the world is wonderful, a flower is beautify and the sound of a waterfall a symphony. Wendell Berry does this often in his writing and poetry, and his quote listed above is one of these prophetic reminders. "The world is a holy vision, had we clarity to see it."

Yet beauty for beauty's sake is one thing, but there is a reason behind the beauty, and it is what makes it holy. Throughout the creation narrative recorded in Genesis chapter one the author depicts God as looking at what he made and remarking to himself that what he made was good. Five times God remarks about the quality of his creation. Finally when his creative work is accomplished he looks over everything and announces that, "It was very good." The goodness involved not only the sum total of his good creations, but also the interplay between them and the remarkable way in which they coexist interdependently. Each necessary for the others. God made the world in harmonious tune, and could not help put proclaim the exceeding worth he placed in it.

The goodness of the creation was more than its sum, or the interconnectedness within it, but also because it was intrinsically good. It was good in relation to God. God's glory was manifest in the harmony and worth he invested in them.

We have to admit that the introduction of sin by humans diminished the harmony of the created order, but we also need to remember who the creator is. Our failures never trump God's successes. In fact he has promised to redeem the creation and mankind with it, making all things new.

The world around us, filled with beauty stands as a reminder of the creator. Its magnificence is a reminder of the magnificence of God and is a pale shadow in comparison. When we stand awestruck by the splendor in nature, let it be a holy vision reminding us of the splendor of God.

Discussion Questions:

- ❖ How often do you remember to really look at the world around you?
- ❖ Describe a time when you were awestruck by something in creation?
- ❖ How does the beauty of creation relate to the beauty and goodness of God?

Prayer:

We pray, oh God, that we can catch a glimpse of your splendor in your creation. Help us to be ever mindful that this holy vision that you have created is in our care and must be handled properly. Forgive us for how we destroy it, heal it and heal us by making all things new.

Glory be to the Father, and to the Son, and to the Holy Spirit.
As it was in the beginning, is now and ever shall ever be, world without end.
Alleluia.
Amen.

DAY SEVENTEEN: AS WE ARE

"...the advent of Christ was made possible by God's love for the world – not God's love for Heaven or for the world as it might be but for the world as it was and is."

The Art of the Commonplace, "Christianity and the Survival of Creation," 308.

Little children, I am with you only a little longer. You will look for me; and as I said to the Jews so now I say to you, 'Where I am going, you cannot come.' I give you a new commandment, that you love one another. Just as I have loved you, you also should love one another. By this everyone will know that you are my disciples, if you have love for one another.

-John 13:33-35 NRSV-

Jesus tells the Disciples that he is about to go to a place where they cannot go. Jesus has just dismissed Judas to betray him, and meanwhile Jesus gives some final instructions to the Disciples before his death. He knows that they will look for him and will not find him, so he gives them a new place to look for him – in their love for one another.

I doubt that the Disciples understood what Jesus was saying, because they never seem to get anything Jesus says until later. Jesus does not just tell them to love one another and leave them to their own imaginations of what that might mean; Jesus has shown them this love all along.

Wendell Berry notes that the love that made the Incarnation happen was a love for the world as it was. He reminds us that when God took a step back and looked at what had been created, God found it beautiful and called it *good*. By calling Creation good throughout Genesis 1, God placed a blessing upon it, saying that it had beauty and lovability before humans ever entered the story.

I wonder if we get what Jesus was saying, even today. We know we are called to love our neighbors, who form one part of the whole Creation, but what does that look like? Jesus showed us by coming to earth for his own enemies, so that we might be brought into right relationship with God.

Perhaps we can begin to extend that love to others when we love them for who they are and not for who we wish they could be. Imagine how deep our sense of community could be when we see one another, scars and bruises and all, call one another *good*, and love one another just the same.

Discussion:

- ❖ What does it mean to you today that God calls all of Creation, including you, good? What does it mean to you today that God calls other members of the human race good? How might we begin to show others the love that Christ has shown us this week?
- ❖ In 1 John 2:7-17, John reminds the believers, whom he addresses as "children" and "Beloved," the words by which Jesus addressed the Disciples, that the command of love is not a new one, but one they have received from the beginning, and an indication of the light that is within them. What does it mean that loving one another means that we are living in the light?

Prayer:

Creator God who makes all things good, remind me today that I am your child, crafted in your image, and that you send me out to share with others the love that you have shared with me. Help me to accept your love for me and to extend that love to those whom I meet today. Amen.

DAY EIGHTEEN: SACRED SPACES

"There are no unsacred places; there are only sacred places and desecrated places."
New Collected Poems, "How to be a Poet," 354.

Then he said, 'Come no closer! Remove the sandals from your feet, for the place on which you are standing is holy ground.'
-Exodus 3:5 NRSV-

We tend to think that Moses' burning bush experience is a holy one, and rightly so. We tend to view calling as a holy thing, and rightly so. So what is it about the ground on which Moses stood that God called holy? Is it the holiness of the calling that happened there? Is it the presence of the Divine?

Moses was keeping the flock of his father-in-law that day when the angel of the LORD appeared to him. It was just an average, ordinary day, leading the flock to pasture at the foot of the mountain of God. In the midst of the average and ordinary, the extraordinary broke in, forever shattering Moses' sense of average and ordinary.

What are the things that you consider to be the most average and ordinary occurrences in your day? Going to the grocery store. Getting the mail. Driving to school or work. Baseball practice. Soccer practice. Play practice. Running around with your children in the backyard. Taking an evening stroll. Standing in line at a restaurant. All of these things are very ordinary in our society, and they happen in very common, ordinary places.

What if we were to begin seeing the places where we do daily, ordinary activities as holy places? There was no place more ordinary for Moses than the pasture where his flocks grazed. There is no place more ordinary for us than the spaces where we spend most of our time. I wonder, though, just how much these spaces have to teach us about life, God, and one another if we have open eyes to see and open ears to hear.

Every space has the capacity to be a sacred space. A hospital room, an urban backyard garden, a classroom, a chapel. Is it what we do or do not do in that space that makes it sacred? Perhaps. Or perhaps there is more. Perhaps it is how we perceive that place, how we treat it, honor it, bless it, and let it bless us. The beginning of a place being desecrated is our inability to see it as sacred. When we become open to the holiness around us, these desecrated spaces can become sacred once again. May we make space in our hearts today to allow the extraordinary to break into our sense of average and ordinary.

Discussion:
- ❖ What are some spaces that you consider sacred? Why are they sacred to you? What are places you consider desecrated? How can they be redeemed?
- ❖ Has there been a time recently when the extraordinary broke into your sense of average and ordinary?
- ❖ Challenge:
- ❖ Walk outside today, and truly look and listen. What might the sacred space of nature be saying to you?

Prayer:
God, help me to understand the power that I have in my perception alone. Help me to see the sacredness in every space you have created. Help me to find beauty where there is pain. Help me to seek healing where there is brokenness. Help me to work toward peace where there is conflict. In all places, help me to see you. Amen.

DAY NINETEEN: A SYSTEM OF BROKENNESS

"A mind cast loose
in whim and greed makes
nature its mirror, and the garden
falls with the man."
New Collected Poems, "Where," 206.

And to the man [God] said, "Because you have listened to the voice of your wife, and have eaten of the tree about which I commanded you, 'You shall not eat of it,' cursed is the ground because of you; in toil you shall eat of it all the days of your life; thorns and thistles it shall bring forth for you; and you shall eat the plants of the field. By the sweat of your face you shall eat bread until you return to the ground, for out of it you were taken; you are dust, and to dust you shall return."

-Genesis 3:17-19 NRSV-

  Often when we think of our sin and its consequences, we think only in terms of our personal wrongdoings and how those choices hurt us or God. The season of Lent is a unique time, however, because we journey through this season together as a church. When we think of what Jesus did on the cross, we are reminded that it was not just for me, but for everybody.

  We also realize that our choices have far-reaching effects for ourselves, other humans, and even creation itself. Sin is not simply a bad choice. Sin affects every level of society, from the personal to communal. Oppressive governments, neighborhoods that don't offer recycling, greedy businesses who exploit people for profit, communities that don't take care of their members who need help, agriculture that pollutes the land and air with chemicals – all of these are examples of systems that have been corrupted by sin. The good news is that just as sin affects the whole world and not just individual humans, God's love is big enough to redeem all of creation.

Discussion Questions:

- ❖ Where do you see systems of oppression, selfishness, or corruption at work in your community?
- ❖ How to you contribute to or at least allow these systems to continue?
- ❖ If you could pick one of these systems to change today, which would it be? What is one thing you can do this week to either raise awareness about this issue or begin changing it?

Prayer:

Lord, have mercy on me, for I am a sinner when I ignore those who need to know your love, when I am too busy to listen for your voice, or when I take more than I need from the earth without any care for its well-being. Have mercy on your church, for we sin when we ignore those who need to know your love, when we are quiet in the face of injustice, or when we allow the noise of our divisions to our purpose. Continue to transform us with your Spirit, so we may be empowered to do your will in our church and communities together.

DAY TWENTY: LIFE, DEATH AND PROVISION

"He is a wilderness looking out at the wild."
New Collected Poems, "Window Poems," 5. 87.

Now, since the Amalekites and the Canaanites live in the valleys, turn tomorrow and set out for the wilderness by the way to the Red Sea.

-Numbers 14:25 NRS-

The wilderness in scripture is a place of hardship, but also place of provision and closeness with God. Prior to this passage the people of Israel had been delivered from Egypt through the miraculous hand of God, but when they reached the boarders of the promised land their hearts quailed at the bad report from the majority of their spies. They rebelled against Moses and the Lord, and they were sentenced to wander forty years in the wilderness. In this verse, the people of Israel stand on the brink of the wilderness, commanded and condemned to enter it.

The wilderness was a place of death. It was unable to sustain the population of the Israelites, and so they had to depend on the God they had just spurned. The entire generation over twenty was condemned to die in their wandering.

Yet it was also a place of life. God sustained even this rebellious people in the inhospitable landscape. In fact, Nehemiah 9:21 tells us that they lacked nothing, and even their clothes did not wear out. After their time was completed he brought them to a provisioned land.

While we may not all live next to a "wilderness," we have all seen or encountered it in some fashion. Wendell Berry reminds us there is even a wilderness inside us. A place where we realize our deep need. There is inside of us the realization that our best in not enough. In this place we can realize our dependence on God, and his plan for us to live with others mutually supporting one another, in our dependence on God. And through it we can encounter the wild, providing, creator God.

Discussion Questions:

When we encounter the wilderness either physical, spiritual or both we encounter a crisis. David Bosch claims, that "crisis is the point where danger and opportunity meet."[3] Reflect on one of your wilderness experiences, a time when you realized your best was not enough and you had to depend on God and others.

❖ How did you react in this situation?
❖ Did you draw closer to God through this difficult experience?
❖ What can you do in the future when this occurs to seek God's provision?

Prayer:

We pray, oh God, for your abundant provision. You sustain life, in the desert, and in the wild places of the world. We pray that you sustain and grow life in the wild places of our hearts.

Glory be to the Father, and to the Son, and to the Holy Spirit.
As it was in the beginning, is now and ever shall ever be, world without end.
Alleluia. Amen.

---

[3] David J. Bosch, *Transforming Mission: Paradigm Shifts in Theology of Mission.* Maryknoll, Orbis: 1991, 7.

Health and Good Work

CHALLENGE:

This week we will begin to consider how our food, habits, body, spirit, work, and community are all connected. As you reflect on these devotions, you may notice several areas in your life where you could make healthier changes, but doing so can be overwhelming. Instead of trying to change everything at once, pick one area on which you would like to focus. Maybe you will choose to cook the majority of your dinners at home this week instead of eating processed food, or maybe you will choose to change something about how you interact with people at work. Whatever it is, write it down and place it somewhere you can see so that you can devote yourself to making this change for the whole week.

DAY TWENTY-ONE: TRUE HAPPINESS

"...we are entirely and helplessly dependent for our happiness on an economy that abuses us along with everything else."
The Art of the Commonplace, "Sex, Economy, Freedom, and Community," 164.

The earth dries up and withers, the world languishes and withers, the heavens languish with the earth. The earth is defiled by its people; they have disobeyed the laws, violated the statutes and broken the everlasting covenant.

-Isaiah 24:4-5 NIV-

Happiness is something that every human desires, and most of what we do in our lives is an attempt to attain it. We work hard at our jobs for the hope of vacation, success, wealth; all things that we are convinced bring about true happiness. We are told that we can find contentment in the newest device, the latest trend, or how quickly we can receive our food. Convenience has become the ideal.

However, in our path to finding happiness we often fool ourselves into thinking that the end justifies our means. We turn a blind eye to the exploitation of people, animals, and especially our land. Any negative ramifications in our pursuit of happiness are simply ignored. It's not until these negative effects hit us personally that we begin to realize that the road to our happiness was misguided.

For instance, if we were to give the example of the state of agriculture in America we see a trail of negative outcomes. We have a variety of companies and manufacturers who have exhausted the land of its resources, mistreated livestock, and put honest farmers out of a job, all for the sake of convenience and our perceived happiness. This is the reality we are tied to in our economy. As Berry rightly states, we are tied to "an economy that abuses us along with everything else."

So how does this relate to who we are as Christians? As God's children we have been given the task of being good stewards of His creation. When we abuse the earth we are in turn abusing ourselves. Our abuse of these things is a result of thinking that our happiness is dependent on what we can take from earth and at what speed or quantity. However, we achieve true happiness only by our obedience to the covenant relationship we have with God and the land he has given us.

Discussion Questions:

- ❖ In what ways do you think we abuse ourselves when we abuse the earth?
- ❖ Why do you think so many Americans turn a blind eye to the exploitation that takes place in our country? How can we build awareness of these problems?
- ❖ How can we begin to combat our reliance on an abusive economy?

Prayer:

God, we ask that You daily remind us that our true happiness is found in You and Your Son Jesus Christ. Help us to be good stewards of Your creation as we seek to honor You with our lives. Give us a heart for the whole of creation as we come alongside You in the redemption of the world. Amen.

DAY TWENTY-TWO: SINGING A WORK SONG

"If it is to be done,
not of the body, not of the will
the strength will come,
but of the delight that moves
lovers in their loves,
that moves the sun and stars,
that stirs the leaf, and lifts the hawk in flight."
New Collected Poems, "From the Crest," 221.

Above all, clothe yourselves with love, which binds everything together in perfect harmony. And let the peace of Christ rule in your hearts, to which indeed you were called in the one body. And be thankful. Let the word of Christ dwell in you richly; teach and admonish one another in all wisdom; and with gratitude in your hearts sing psalms, hymns, and spiritual songs to God. And whatever you do, in word or deed, do everything in the name of the Lord Jesus, giving thanks to God the Father through him.
-Colossians 3:14-17 NRSV-

"Work" is not a word that we typically use in a positive way. Work is what we do to make money so we can do the things we actually want to do. Work is what someone tells us that we have to do. We work in the office, we study homework for school, and we do chores when we come home. Taking care of our families, land, and community is work, too. We work *all* the time. But what if we could reclaim "work"?

Berry encourages us not to think of work as drudgery, but as an art. What if we did our work out of love and delight for those we were serving and for the God who has called us to do it? Maybe then our work could turn into a song, something beautiful that could move others to do the same.

Discussion Questions:

- ❖ What are aspects that you dislike about your work?

- ❖ What are aspects that you like about your work?

- ❖ What motivates you to do good work? How does your work benefit people you care about?

Prayer:

To Creator God,
whose hands worked to form us and continue to sustain us; through Jesus Christ, whose work of love and forgiveness teaches us how to be human; and in the Holy Spirit, who continues to be at work transforming us and the world, we pray that our work will glorify you and make your love known to all whom we meet and serve in the midst of it.
Amen.

DAY TWENTY-THREE: MEANINGFUL WORK

"Work connects us both to creation and to eternity. This is the reason for Mother Ann Lee's famous instruction: 'Do all your work as though you had a thousand years to live on earth, and as you would if you knew you must die tomorrow.'"

The Art of the Commonplace, "Christianity and the Survival of Creation," 316.

Whatever you do, work at it with all your heart, as working for the Lord, not for human masters.

- Colossians 3:23 NIV-

Work is something that it typically equated with drudgery in today's world, and many people tend to avoid it as much as possible. Recreation and relaxation has become the greatest desire, leaving a sour connotation for the work even if it is meaningful work. It is easy in today's society to view our work and our labors as futile, because we ask ourselves how our work has any meaning for the future. A man working a nine to five desk job might fail to see how his work is meaningful or how he is advancing God's Kingdom. Our society has led him to believe that work is merely a means to an end, that end being recreation or relaxation.

This is the type of mentality that Wendell Berry is vehemently against. He sees the importance in good, hard, honest work, and how it can be far more meaningful than our moments of relaxation and recreation. For instance, what are the moments in your life that remember the most? Are they the moments when you vegged out on a Saturday and watched a couple movies? Or was it that the time where you engaged in meaningful work with a group of people seeking a common goal? Surprisingly enough, we often remember the latter rather than the former.

As Christians, we should always believe that our work has a purpose, that there can be actual fruits of our labor. Even in the menial tasks of life, God is working and moving through us to bring about His good. With this realization, our work takes on a brand new meaning. We are no longer tied to the idea that work should be something to avoid, but rather we are free to honor and glorify the Lord through our work.

Colossians 3:23 instructs believers to do their work diligently, but it also gives ultimate direction for *who* we do the work for. It's made clear in this verse that we should work for God's glory, not for the approval of man. This drastically changes how we are able to approach our work. So for the man with the 9-5 desk job this means that he can begin his day by acknowledging God as master of the workplace. His day's work would be in pursuit of aims that honor and glorify.

Only when we view our work in light of bringing God glory do we truly remove the drudgery from it. Viewing our work as an opportunity to build God's Kingdom truly "connect us both to creation and to eternity."

Discussion Questions:

- ❖ In what ways have you experienced meaningful work in your life? Share that moment with others and reflect on what made it meaningful?
- ❖ What prevents you from attaining a sense of purpose in your work?
- ❖ What ways can you begin to allow the glory of God become the driving force being your work?

Prayer:

Lord, give us purpose and direction in our work. Help us engage in meaningful work, forever seeking Your glory in the day's daily tasks. Help us be connected both creation and eternity. Amen.

DAY TWENTY-FOUR: BECOMING WHOLE

"We lose our health — and create profitable diseases and dependences — by failing to see the direct connections between living and eating, eating and working, working and loving. In gardening, for instance, one works with the body to feed the body. The work, if it is knowledgeable, makes for excellent food. And it makes one hungry. The work thus makes eating both nourishing and joyful, not consumptive..."
The Art of the Commonplace, "The Body and the Earth," 132.

I will take you from the nations, and gather you from all the countries, and bring you into your own land. I will sprinkle clean water upon you, and you shall be clean from all your uncleannesses, and from all your idols I will cleanse you. A new heart I will give you, and a new spirit I will put within you; and I will remove from your body the heart of stone and give you a heart of flesh. I will put my spirit within you, and make you follow my statutes and be careful to observe my ordinances. Then you shall live in the land that I gave to your ancestors; and you shall be my people, and I will be your God. I will save you from all your uncleannesses, and I will summon the grain and make it abundant and lay no famine upon you. I will make the fruit of the tree and the produce of the field abundant, so that you may never again suffer the disgrace of famine among the nations.
-Ezekiel 36:24-30 NRSV-

During Lent we often think about giving things up — chocolate, soda, cigarettes, etc. — as a way of remember Christ's suffering. However, Christ saves us in order to make us whole and to teach us how to be fully human so that we can live the kind of life that God intended us to have. God promises to put a new spirit in us so that we can live abundantly in a way that gives glory to God.

Perhaps instead of meditating on what we should exclude during Lent, we should meditate on how we can live wholly and fully as the people God created us to be. This might mean adding things like healthy food grown in your community, time for a hobby that refreshes you, or more reflection on Scripture rather than simply taking something out of your life.

Discussion Questions:

- ❖ What are some healthy interests or habits that make you feel more alive?
- ❖ What can you change about your routine in order to incorporate more of these activities?
- ❖ How can you think about living, eating, working, and loving in a way that recognizes that all of these are interconnected? If you're missing a component, which one is it, and what can you do to reclaim it?

Prayer:

Creator God, we know that you created the whole world, and we thank you for its many blessings. We pray that you will renew us with your Spirit and teach us to honor you in how we get our food, what we eat, how we work, and how we share your love. Amen.

DAY TWENTY-FIVE: FUEL FOR FELLOWSHIP

"I have taken in the light
that quickened eye and leaf.
May my brain be bright with praise
of what I eat, in the brief blaze
of motion and of thought.
May I be worthy of my meat."
New Collected Poems, "Prayer After Eating," 169.

Day by day, as they spent much time together in the temple, they broke bread at home and ate their food with glad and generous hearts, praising God and having the goodwill of all the people. And day by day the Lord added to their number those who were being saved.

-Acts 2:46-47 NRSV-

What is the first thing that comes to mind when you think about food? Maybe it's the latest TV commercial for a new burger or restaurant. Maybe it's a tradition, like eating hot wings while watching football or devouring pumpkin pie after Thanksgiving dinner. Our culture affects how we view food, and often not for the best. Food is associated with entertainment, pleasure, and consumption. On the other hand, food also is viewed as something that needs to be restricted in order to lose weight and achieve a certain body image. But what is the real purpose of food?

In this poem, Berry challenges us not to think of food as valuable because of how good it tastes or how much we can eat. Food is a gift. It has an intrinsic worth because it comes from something – whether a plant or animal – that God created. Eating it, therefore, is not just a gift but a responsibility.

Food is fuel so that we may be a gift to others. If we viewed food as a nutrient source that enabled us to go and serve God and our neighbors, would that change what we ate and what we did after eating? We often end prayers with the phrase, "Bless this food to the nourishment of our bodies," but what if we sought to use the food to nourish not just ourselves but also our communities?

In Acts, we see that the disciples in the early church community enjoyed coming together and sharing a meal with each other, but while doing so they did not forget about other people in their community or their responsibility to spread the good news of God's love revealed in Christ.

Eating should be pleasurable because it reminds us that God created the world and continues to provide for us, but it shouldn't end there. Good food should not go to waste. We should be "worthy" of our food by using the nourishment we receive to share God's love with our community.

Discussion Questions:

- ❖ Does this poem change the way you think about your food?
- ❖ What's your initial reaction to the final line, "May I be worthy of my meat"?
- ❖ What can you do to show more appreciation for the food you have? Some examples might be buying from local farmers, eating less processed food, or purchasing ethically raised meat.

Prayer:

Write your own prayer in the space below *after* your next meal.

DAY TWENTY-SIX: A HOLY WAITING

"Perhaps it is only when we focus our minds on our machines that time seems short."

Art of the Common Place "People, Land and Community." 192.

But do not ignore this one fact, beloved, that with the Lord one day is like a thousand years, and a thousand years are like one day. The Lord is not slow about his promise, as some think of slowness, but is patient with you, not wanting any to perish, but all to come to repentance. But the day of the Lord will come like a thief, and then the heavens will pass away with a loud noise, and the elements will be dissolved with fire, and the earth and everything that is done on it will be disclosed. Since all these things are to be dissolved in this way, what sort of persons ought you to be in leading lives of holiness and godliness?

-2 Peter 3:8-11 NRS-

"I don't have time," is a phrase we use so often that it becomes a normal part of our day or week. Yet the absurdity of this statement is only visible to common sense. No matter how we perceive the length of our days, their uniformity is only differentiated by the amount of light the day contains. Each day, no matter how it feels contains twenty-four hours. The shortness of our time is a product of what we do with it.

Wendell Berry, in his typical prophetic fashion, reminds us that our time simply seems short because we have filled it with distractions. 2 Peter reminds us that our lack of time and impatience is a symptom, and does not come from God's design. Our day may feel like just a second, but to God a thousand years is like a day.

The people 2 Peter was written to were concerned with the fact that Jesus had not returned as soon as they thought he would. They were beginning to suspect he would not come back at all. This reference served as a reminder that God does not renege on his promises. His patience is purposeful. He is giving us time to repent and call others to join us.

Yet we so often fill our hours, days and weeks with distractions. How many hours do we spend watching T.V., on our phones, or staring at computer screens? We waste our God given time on nonessential distractions and entertainment. Yet we are not promised even an hour. This passage describes God's return as a thief. This is inherently negative terminology. To apply this negative term to God, the author must be emphasizing something strongly. The emphasis is on the unexpectedness of Christ's return. A thief comes only when least expected, otherwise they would be thwarted. For the author to apply the negative image of a thief to God, he must truly believe that God will come when we least expect it. This element of surprise, should not lead to unhealthy anxiety, but rather to hope of imminent return and prepared living. The best thing we can do is exactly what the author of 2 Peter says "lead lives of holiness and godliness." Only by using our precious hours and days in pursuit of these holy endeavors, can we be prepared for Christ's return.

Discussion Questions:
- ❖ On what do you spend the largest portion of your time? (outside of sleep)
- ❖ What are some ways in which you could use your time better?
- ❖ How do you cultivate a life of holiness and godliness? What are some practical steps to realize this?

Prayer:

>We pray, oh God, for patience like yours, accepting the difficulties that accompany it. We pray that we use the hours you give us with purpose and wisdom. Forgive us for the ones we have wasted. Mold our hours so that we are transformed into your likeness.

>Glory be to the Father, and to the Son, and to the Holy Spirit.
>As it was in the beginning, is now and ever shall ever be, world without end.
>Alleluia.
>Amen.

Economy and Government

CHALLENGE:

Have ever considered how your spending habits reflect your view of creation care? Throughout this section of devotions we will be discussing the Economy and our place in it. This week, find one item from every room in your home that you do not need. Make a pile, give thanks to God that you have all that you need, and give it away to share with someone else.

DAY TWENTY-SEVEN: THE SPIRIT WITHIN ALL OF US

"...we and all other creatures live by a sanctity that is inexpressibly intimate, for to every creature, the gift of life is a portion of the breath and spirit of God."

-*The Art of the Commonplace*, "Christianity and the Survival of Creation," 308.

Then the LORD God formed man from the dust of the ground, and breathed into his nostrils the breath of life; and the man became a living being.

-Genesis 2:7 NRSV-

When our culture thinks of the worth of a person, we tend to think about an amount. We ask, "How much is that person worth?" We consider financial income, personal achievements, assets, and the like. We measure success by the things one has acquired. But what if there is more to it than that?

To be alive, to have air coming through our noses and blood pumping through our veins, is to be constantly breathing the very spirit of God. We are no different than Adam; we too have been formed from dust by the gentle hands of a loving God. It is only when God breathes into our nostrils that we experience life.

If all people hold this one thing in common, then we share the most intimate and sacred part of our lives — our life itself. To all be created in the image of God, crafted in our own unique individuality, and to be alive is to hold within our being the very Spirit of God, the same Spirit that is in every other human being who walks the earth.

How would the world change if we began to see those around us as people who carry with them the breath of God? Would we treat our neighbors differently? Our enemies? How would the way we view war, violence, capital punishment, and the like change if we saw one another as our brothers and sisters who carry in them the same breath that is in us?

As we live and move and have our being in the Spirit of God, may we be people who acknowledge that Spirit in one another and in those with whom we come into contact daily. May we treat each moment with others as the sacred encounter that it is, as a meeting between the Spirit of God in you and the Spirit of God in me.

Discussion:

- ❖ How would our lives be different if we treated others as persons who carry the breath of God?
- ❖ How would seeing others in this way help us to become more fully human?

Prayer:

God, you have crafted each individual uniquely and given each of us a portion of your Spirit. Help us to acknowledge your Spirit both in ourselves and in one another. Teach us what it means to honor that inexpressibly intimate sanctity that we all share. Amen.

DAY TWENTY-EIGHT: NEW RULES

"Rats and roaches live by competition under the law of supply and demand; it is the privilege of human beings to live under the laws of justice and mercy."

The Art of the Commonplace, "Economy & Pleasure," 212

He has told you, O mortal, what is good; and what does the LORD require of you but to do justice, and to love kindness, and to walk humbly with your God?

-Micah 6:8 NRSV-

In the movie Ratatouille, a rat named Remy has a dream of becoming a chef. He knows that in the fine city of Paris, France, humans do not always sit well with the idea of a rat in the kitchen. He goes through a series of experiences and ends up leading a young man, Alfredo Linguini, who wants to be a chef but is no good, to make wonderful dishes at a famous Parisian restaurant.

There is a scene in the movie in which Remy returns to the sewer and is met by an old friend. The rat is huge, after living his life in the sewers, scrounging for food in garbage collections. He encourages Remy to return with him to his old way of life, but Remy does not want to abandon his newfound love of cooking, eating, and being with the humans.

Remy has found a place in society where, though very secret, he is loved and cared for, though he is a rat. His friend Alfredo has given him a place to live and to exercise his love of cooking. The boundaries that usually exist between rats and humans have been torn down, and a true friendship is growing.

God speaks through the prophet Micah that what God longs for is not our sacrifice or obedience to rules about cleanliness; what God wants is for us to do rightly, to love being kind to one another, and to humbly join God on the journey of redemption, restoration, and transformation.

In the movie Ratatouille, Alfredo works against the rules (even rules about cleanliness) in the name of relationship and love. Though the movie is fictional and unrealistic, it paints a picture of the Kingdom of God. We are to be less worried about the rules and more worried about doing what is right, loving one another, and walking with God. That is all God requires.

When we live under the rules of justice, kindness, and mercy, not only are we changed, but so is the world around us. In a society that lives under rules of supply and demand, people expect us to constantly compete and to never be satisfied with what we have. May we be people of surprise. May we surprise those around us with the beautiful mercy of our Savior, as we extend to others the precious gift that has been so freely given to us.

Discussion:

- ❖ What if we were to surprise others by living under the laws of justice and mercy rather than of supply and demand? How would individual lives be changed? How would society be changed?
- ❖ What is our place as individuals and as communities of faith in bringing about systemic justice in our society?

Prayer:

God, help me to realize places in my life where I am living more out of the laws of supply and demand than of love, grace, and restoration. In those places within me, remind me of the love and grace you have extended to me, and help me to faithfully share these gifts with others. Amen.

DAY TWENTY-NINE: KINGS AND KINGDOMS

"Denounce the government and embrace
the flag. Hope to live in that free
republic for which it stands."

> *New Collected Poems "Manifesto: The Mad Farmer Liberation Front." 173.*

Then Pilate entered the headquarters again, summoned Jesus, and asked him, "Are you the King of the Jews?" Jesus answered, "Do you ask this on your own, or did others tell you about me?" Pilate replied, "I am not a Jew, am I? Your own nation and the chief priests have handed you over to me. What have you done?" Jesus answered, "My kingdom is not from this world. If my kingdom were from this world, my followers would be fighting to keep me from being handed over to the Jews. But as it is, my kingdom is not from here." Pilate asked him, "So you are a king?" Jesus answered, "You say that I am a king. For this I was born, and for this I came into the world, to testify to the truth. Everyone who belongs to the truth listens to my voice.

-John 18:33-37 NRS-

In the U.S. we are afforded the privilege of separating the state from the church. The creation of such a condition is the direct result of religious denominations and groups who did not possess this liberty elsewhere, and were persecuted or mistreated for their beliefs. When the opportunity for a new start was available religious leaders were keen to make sure the state said out of the church. To accomplish this no religious group was allowed to receive favorable conditions from the government, because it could lead to a state church, which was intolerable to many of the colonists. Religious liberty was a vital part of the new republic.

A major issue that we face today, is that many in churches have forgotten this early lesson on freedom. Many groups who once ardently fought for separating the church and the state, now clamber to be favored by the state. There is much wailing that America is no longer a Christian nation. The issue with this is that America was never a Christian nation. It was never supposed to be. It was supposed to be a free nation, in which all could freely practice their faith without government interference.

Jesus' words to Pilate in this passage speak prophetically to any notion of "going back to a Christian nation." In the moment of triumphant weakness, in the hands of an oppressive nation, Jesus proclaims his kingship by denouncing an earthly kingdom. "My kingdom is not from this world."

Wendell Berry reminds us that the government under which we live is just as imperfect as Rome was in Jesus' day. Identifying one political party as the *Christian* party, is simply unchristian. Being a Christian does not force one to vote for one party or another. Being Christian forces us to vote for people who will uphold the ideals of liberty which can enable us to serve our true king. Denounce the government! Such strong words remind me of Jesus' actions in the Temple in Jerusalem in which he threw over the tables of economic exploitation, and reminded the people of its true purpose. So we too need to recognize that our government is not what we are loyal too; we are loyal to the liberty for which our flag stands.

Ultimately it is most important to remember that all governments are transitory, including the U.S. They are not supreme in power, or liberty. In the end, the "kingdom that is not from this world" will break into this world in its fullness and true peace will come over the land. With this in mind we must always remember where our true loyalties lie and what it means to be a citizen of the Kingdom of God.

Discussion Questions:

- ❖ In what ways does our faith effect our political views?
- ❖ What does it mean to be part of the Kingdom of God?
- ❖ How would someone "denounce the government and embrace the flag" practically in life? What could this look like?

Prayer:

We pray, oh God, for your kingdom to come, and for your will to be done, on earth as it is in heaven. Let our lives be a witness to your kingdom, and the peace it brings.

Glory be to the Father, and to the Son, and to the Holy Spirit.
As it was in the beginning, is now and ever shall ever be, world without end.
Alleluia.
Amen.

DAY THIRTY: WHOSE WORLD IS IT, ANYWAY?

"It is hardly surprising, then, that there should be some profound resemblances between our treatment of our bodies and our treatment of the earth"

The Art of the Commonplace, "The Body and the Earth," 93.

The earth is the Lord's, and everything in it. The world and all its people belong to him.

-Psalm 24:1-

  Have you ever stopped to think about how we as humans relate to the created world we live in? Often times we let the world around us fade into the background as we get caught up in the busyness of life. However, by our failure to acknowledge the world around us, creation suffers. Forests are being cleared for building projects, our lakes and rivers are riddled with garbage, and the land around us is destroyed by poor agricultural practices. Can we truly say that this is ideal?

  Whether we like it or not our entire being is tied to the world around us. We rely on trees for clean oxygen, rivers and lakes for water, and the farmland around us for food. It is easy for one to see the lasting effects of failing to be good stewards of the land. This does not only affect the land itself, but in turn affects our health, economy, and vitality. However, more so than not, humans fail to see the "resemblances between our treatment of our bodies and our treatment of the earth."

  However, one could take Berry's quote further by stating that our treatment of creation shows a lack of care towards what God wills for His people. By mistreating the earth we not only mistreat our bodies in the process, we are ultimately reflecting a mistreatment of what calls His people to be: good stewards. As Christians we are called to good stewards of God's creation, reflecting our love for Him back into everything He has provided for us.

In order for Christians to better understand their role in creation-care we must constantly remind ourselves of God's sovereignty over the earth. Psalm 24:1 answers the question, "Whose world is It, anyway?" Simply put, the earth is the Lord's. Not the property of humans, agricultural entities, or industries, but the Lord's. With this in mind one can begin to understand the importance of caring for the earth. By doing so we are not only creating a healthier life for all of humanity, we are serving our Creator!

Discussion:

- ❖ Do you agree with Wendell Berry's quote? In what ways do you see the mistreatment of the earth reflect the treatment of our bodies?
- ❖ What are some ways you could promote good stewardship of creation in your life today?
- ❖ Can you think of a time where you saw God's beauty in His creation? Discuss that experience. How can what you experienced lead you to action regarding creation care?

Prayer:

Sovereign God we come to You humbled, acknowledging You as our loving Creator. Help us see Your face in creation today as we seek to bring You glory through our stewardship. Amen.

DAY THIRTY-ONE: FOR FREEDOM

"We who prayed and wept for liberty from kings and the yoke of liberty accept the tyranny of things we do not need. In plentitude too free, we have become adept beneath the yoke of greed."
New Collected Poems, "We Who Prayed and Wept," 245.

Then the LORD said, 'I have observed the misery of my people who are in Egypt; I have heard their cry on account of their taskmasters. Indeed, I know their sufferings, and I have come down to deliver them from the Egyptians, and to bring them up out of that land to a good and broad land, a land flowing with milk and honey, to the country of the Canaanites, the Hittites, the Amorites, the Perizzites, the Hivites, and the Jebusites.
-Exodus 3:7-8 NRSV-

Can you imagine being part of one of the first families to come to the Americas from Europe? Imagine feeling so oppressed by the government that it would be worth risking the lives of your entire family in order to travel toward the hope of a new land of freedom. You would leave behind the comforts of familiarity and any belongings that would not fit in your suitcase. You would never see home again, and it would not be certain what your new one would become.

Now imagine being one of the forefathers and mothers, standing in parliament, begging for the freedom of your people, and being rejected time and again. You would fight long and hard, with solid arguments and great fervor, but to no avail.

Imagine then being Moses. You would stand before Pharaoh, shaking in your shoes, no doubt, but certain of God's call for you to be there. You would go before Pharaoh time and time again, hear Pharaoh say no, then when a plague comes, yes, and then no again. You would cry out to God, and God would hear you. Finally, God would say, "Get up, prepare the Passover meal, and eat it with your loins girded and with haste, because I am coming." And you would lead your people out of slavery by night.

Imagine then surrendering all of that hard-fought freedom to a new oppressor, because you are not quite sure how to live life without being under the bonds of some sort of slavery. You are no longer in physical chains, and so you create for yourself some invisible yoke to which you can belong. You don't know how to stand as a free person; you need someone or something on which you can depend.

It doesn't seem to make sense. Once-oppressed people, set free, now seeking a new slavery, in the form of material possessions that we can hoard in our greed. If we have been truly set free, why then do we remain in bondage to our things? We build factories to make more stuff, because what we have is never enough. We build massive supermarkets where we can buy more stuff, and when we get it home, it is too much, so we build storage buildings to hold our possessions. What if we were to give some of it away? Would we feel freer? Try it, and see.

Discussion Questions:
- ❖ Has there been a time when you fought very hard for something that you eventually received? Could you imagine giving that up, only to belong to the same problem once again?
- ❖ Have you seen evidence that our society is in bondage to possessions? What is the hope of our freedom?

Prayer:
God, thank you for giving me everything I need. Help me to distinguish between that which I need and that which I hoard. Help me to set myself free from possessions by sharing what I have with others. Amen.

DAY THIRTY-TWO: QUANTITY, QUALITY, OR SOMETHING ELSE?

"Calling his neighbors together into the sanctity of their lives separate and together... he cries: Come all ye conservatives and liberals who want to conserve the good things and be free, come away from the merchants of big answers, whose hands are metalled with power; from the union of anywhere and everywhere by the purchase of everything from everybody at the lowest price and the sale of anything to anybody at the highest price; from the union of work and debt, work and despair; from the wage slavery of the helplessly well-employed."

New Collected Poems, "The Mad Farmer, Flying the Rough Branch, Secedes from the Union," 326.

With what shall I come before the LORD, and bow myself before God on high? Shall I come before him with burnt offerings, with calves a year old? Will the LORD be pleased with thousands of rams, with ten thousands of rivers of oil? Shall I give my firstborn for my transgression, the fruit of my body for the sin of my soul?" He has told you, O mortal, what is good; and what does the LORD require of you but to do justice, and to love kindness, and to walk humbly with your God?

-Micah 6:6-8 NRS-

The prophetic message of Micah comes to a head here with this question and answer dialogue. The ultimate question being asked is, "how does one approach God?" The subject that is inquiring asks if a sacrifice is what is necessary to approach God. Since there is no answer that follows, we are left with the distinct impression that the answer is "no."

The imploring person is unperturbed however and pushes on thinking that the issue is a measure of quantity. What if I were to give a vast quantity. The imagery is striking "Thousands of rams, ten-thousands of rivers of oil." If a sacrifice is not enough, what if I give everything I own? Again the non-answer from the text leaves us with the impression that the amount of the sacrifices will not earn God's ear.

The supplicant seems to grow desperate with the continued rejection, and after having offered all worldly possessions, an unthinkable notion rises to his petitioning lips before it can be quelled. "What if I give my child, my firstborn?" What if the depth of the sacrifice is what is needed to enter the presence of God? The prophet speaks up at this point dashing the sacrificial dreams of this listener and exposing the unlistening ear of the person trying to gain the ear of God. "He has told you, O mortal, what is good." It was never a matter or sacrifice. Neither the amount nor the depth of the sacrifice will accomplish its task, since a sacrifice was never what was required.

We live in a culture of excess. We try and achieve peace through war, comfort through distraction, divinity through power, power through wealth. In the poem selection above Wendell Berry reminds us that our collection of wealth and products do not add sanctity to our lives. In fact, he reminds us in strong poetic language, that all we accomplish is the loss of any sense of good work, and the "wage slavery of the helplessly well-employed." More of the wrong things will never add up to anything good.

Both Micah and Berry speak prophetically to our consumer notions that we can buy satisfaction, happiness or even the listening ear of God. God does not say that we are in his good graces simply by giving everything up. He want more than just sacrifice, he wants a living sacrifice that is willing to be transformed by his love so that we can, "do justice, love kindness and walk humbly with our God."

Discussion Questions:

- ❖ Have you ever tried to bargain with God?
- ❖ Do you ever place the emphasis on the wrong thing in terms of faith and church life? (for instance, a list of do's and don'ts)
- ❖ Do you need to rethink the way you approach God?

Prayer:

We pray, oh God, our lives can be living sacrifices, acceptable in your sight. We pray that our actions bring justice and show loving kindness to those around us. Forgive us for our poor attempts to buy your affection. And strengthen us to courageously and humbly walk before you.

Glory be to the Father, and to the Son, and to the Holy Spirit.
As it was in the beginning, is now and ever shall ever be, world without end.
Alleluia.
Amen.

DAY THIRTY-THREE: THE FREEDOM OF LIMITATION

"...we can make ourselves whole only by accepting our partiality, by living within our limits, by being human – not by trying to be gods. By restraint they make themselves whole."

The Art of the Commonplace, "The Use of Energy," 292.

For you know the generous act of our Lord Jesus Christ, that though he was rich, yet for your sakes he became poor, so that by his poverty you might become rich.

-2 Corinthians 8:9 NRSV-

Consumerism. This prevalence of a consumerist attitude affects not only our shopping habits but every aspect of our lives. Most of us consume food throughout the day without any knowledge of where it came from, how it was treated, or how it was grown. Our vehicles consume gas so we can drive to work. Our businesses consume money to make profits, often taking advantage of the very consumers purchasing the products. Our time is consumed with busyness as we hop from one task to another so that we are unable to stop and spend time with the people we love or truly do one thing well and take pleasure in doing good work. When we finally make it home, we are so exhausted by our consuming, all we can do is sit in front of our TVs to consume various forms of entertainment. This is the "American Dream," and the people who succeed in it are the ones who can consume the most.

We are not good at practicing restraint, whether in how much we buy, what we take from others, or in the numerous responsibilities we try to juggle. In doing so, we shove God to the side and try to become gods by accomplishing things on our own and finding fulfillment in whatever stuff we can consume. This is not the kind of life God calls us to lead, however. Being a Christian means following Christ, who humbled himself for the sake of others and laid down his life so that we might have life to the fullest. This kind of richness cannot be measured by material things or earthly success. It is measured by how the Spirit empowers us to love one another and give generously, even when that means accepting our weaknesses and restraining ourselves from desires that hurt one another and do not make us whole.

Questions:
- ❖ In what ways do you try to exceed your limits? How is this harmful?
- ❖ How can you practice restraint, and how might this demonstrate Christ's love for others?

Prayer:
> God, grant me the serenity to accept the things I cannot change,
> The courage to change the things I can,
> And the wisdom to know the difference.
> > - Serenity Prayer, by Reinhold Niebuhr

Death and Resurrection

The silence of God is a reality of life, but it is easy to create a false silence with our noise. Today, intentionally spend some time in silence. It may be helpful to set a timer, so you don't keep checking a clock, and it may be helpful to have a notepad to write down the things that you remember you need to do. The goal is to ease your mind and heart and focus on listening. It may be in the silence of that moment that you hear God calling your name. However, don't be discouraged if you hear nothing. Just remember that God is near, and his love endures forever.

DAY THIRTY-FOUR: REMEMBERING THE COST

"All our years around us, near us,
I saw him furious and narrow,
like most men, and saw the virtue
that made him unlike most.
It was his passion to be true
to the condition of the Fall –
to live by the sweat of his face, to eat
his bread, assured that cost was paid."
　　　　　New Collected Poems, "Elegy," 272.

For there is no distinction, since all have sinned and fall short of the glory of God; they are now justified by his grace as a gift, through the redemption that is in Christ Jesus, whom God put forward as a sacrifice of atonement by his blood, effective through faith. He did this to show his righteousness, because in his divine forbearance he had passed over the sins previously committed; it was to prove at the present time that he himself is righteous and that he justifies the one who has faith in Jesus.
　　　　　　　　　　　　　　　- Romans 3:23-26 NRSV -

　　　　During Holy Week, we remember Christ's suffering and death. Though we would rather jump to the joyous resurrection on Easter morning, Holy Week forces us to pause. We spread ashes on our foreheads as we reflect on our sinfulness and the brokenness of our world. As we read about Jesus' trial and crucifixion, we realize that we are apart of the story. We are the ones shouting, "Crucify him!" We are the ones who deny him. We are the ones who leave the cross lonely and afraid, forgetting God's promises and doubting that the future could possibly bring anything good out of the darkness that presses in on us.

In this poem, Berry imagines a conversation with a friend who has died and looks back over their time together. What strikes Berry about this friend is not his great accomplishments but his character. He was the kind of person who recognized and accepted his limits. He knew his own brokenness, but he also knew the cost was paid. Having such a humble perspective of one's self takes bravery, and it also takes trust in the One who redeems us. This week, let's embrace Holy Week and remember our sinfulness together, and let's not forget just how costly our forgiveness really was.

Questions:

❖ What makes you most uncomfortable about Holy Week?
❖ Where can you best imagine yourself in the story of Jesus' crucifixion – the crowd who shouts for his crucifixion? The disciples? The women watching in the crowd? Somewhere else?
❖ Take time to contemplate whatever scene you find yourself in, then ask what you might learn from it about yourself as you go through Holy Week.

Prayer:

Jesus Christ, who was crucified for all of our sakes, we confess that we do not want to acknowledge our brokenness. We admit that we want the resurrection without the pain. We ask you to give us the courage to face our sinfulness. Remind us that being your disciples means picking up our own crosses and dying to ourselves. Please grace us with the perseverance to walk this journey with you. Amen.

DAY THIRTY-FIVE: HOPING FOR REDEMPTION

"There will be a resurrection of the wild...there will be a second coming of the trees."
New Collected Poems, "Window Poems," 94.

I consider that the sufferings of this present time are not worth comparing with the glory about to be revealed to us. For the creation waits with eager longing for the revealing of the children of God; for the creation was subjected to futility, not of its own will but by the will of the one who subjected it, in hope that the creation itself will be set free from its bondage to decay and will obtain the freedom of the glory of the children of God. We know that the whole creation has been groaning in labor pains until now; and not only the creation, but we ourselves, who have the first fruits of the Spirit, groan inwardly while we wait for adoption, the redemption of our bodies. For in hope we were saved. Now hope that is seen is not hope. For who hopes for what is seen? But if we hope for what we do not see, we wait for it with patience.
-Rom. 8:18-25 NRSV-

We have already spoken of our need for wilderness in order to remind us of our dependence on God and to refresh our spirit. We also have spoken of the destruction that humanity inflicts on wilderness and how our brokenness affects not only other humans, but all of creation. During Lent, we remember Jesus' suffering. This leads us to mourn for our sins and seek to strip away from our lives the things that cause harm so that we can re-center on God. As we draw closer to Good Friday, however, we cannot help but also think of Easter Sunday.

We know that even though Lent involves mourning, that is not the last word. And so we remember that although the gravity of our brokenness is something to take seriously, we have hope in Jesus Christ. Even when we face difficult challenges, we know that these hardships will not last forever. Jesus' death was not the end. Our brokenness is not the end. And creation's groaning is not the end. There will be a second coming of our Lord Jesus Christ, and God's kingdom will be known in all the earth.

Discussion Questions:
- ❖ In what ways do you see creation groaning now?
- ❖ What are some small but practical changes you could make in your daily life to help?
- ❖ Think about a time when you felt like everything was going wrong. What helped you through it? If you feel like that now, where can you turn for encouragement?

Prayer:

Lord, open our ears to hear the groaning of your children and your creation. Give us open hearts and open our hands to respond to those who are hurting. And when we cannot see beyond the darkness of our pain, open our eyes to find hope in the power of your love and promises once more. In Jesus' name we pray, Amen.

DAY THIRTY-SIX: PREPARING FOR A BURIAL

"Where shall a man go who keeps the memories of the dead..."
New Collected Poems, "At a Country Funeral", 184.

While he was in Bethany, reclining at the table in the home of Simon the Leper, a woman came with an alabaster jar of very expensive perfume, made of pure nard. She broke the jar and poured the perfume on his head...

-Mark 14:3 NIV-

As we continue through Holy Week we anxiously await the good news of Christ's Resurrection. The joy of full salvation that comes from Jesus' victory over death stirs in us a feeling of joy and gratitude as we serve our risen Savior. However, as joyous as Resurrection day will be, we must also remember the seriousness of the days leading up to Christ's death on the cross. We do in fact serve a risen savior, but Christ had to humble himself lower still as he bore the weight of our sins on the cross. We must ask ourselves what we can learn from the days leading up to Christ's death and what implications they have for our lives.

Mark's gospel gives an account of a woman who, after entering into a home where Christ and his disciples were dining, broke a jar of expensive perfume on his head. If you are confused by the this woman's act you are not alone. Even the disciples present were appalled by what she had done, claiming that the expensive perfume could have been sold and the money given to the poor. However, Mark notes that instead of scolding the woman Jesus defends and affirms what she had done. Jesus states that what she did was not only a beautiful gesture, but was in preparation for his burial (verse 6 & 8). The woman understood the necessity of her gesture as she understood what Jesus would soon endure in death.

So what can we glean from this woman's actions? Most importantly we see in her an example of someone who was willing to do all that they possibly could for Christ. Her love for Christ outweighed her desire for extravagant things, and her selfless act showed that she was aware that Jesus' death was soon to take place. Are we willing to love others extravagantly, lowering ourselves in humility and self-sacrifice? Are we are of what God is calling us to do at this very time?

Wendell Berry asks in his poem "At a Country Funeral," concerning "where shall a man should go who keeps the memories of the dead…" However, in the context of the days leading up to the death of Christ, one could just as well ask "what shall a man *do* who keeps the memories of the dead?" How does the death of Christ affect our understanding of what he calls us to do in this life? The seriousness of Christ's death on the cross should lead one to both repentance and action. Consider the example of the woman in Mark 14 today; seek to love God extravagantly through your love and care for others.

Discussion Questions:

❖ What is your "expensive perfume" that you need to humbly place at the feet of Jesus?

❖ One of the things that Jesus notes in Mark 14 is the fact that the woman's act was a "timely thing." In what ways have you felt God calling you to a certain action? How do you discern whether or not it is God's timing?

Prayer:

Lord, help me learn from the sacrifice of the woman in Bethany. Let my life be driven by self-sacrifice as I seek to glorify You through my love for others. Amen.

DAY THIRTY-SEVEN: A GIFT FREELY GIVEN

"Outside the window is a roofed wooden tray he fills with seeds for the birds. . . They flirt out with tail or beak and waste more sometimes than they eat. And the man, knowing the price of seed, wishes they would take more care. But they understand only what is free, and he can give only as they will take. Thus they have enlightened him. He buys the seed, to make it free."
New Collected Poems, "Window Poems," 8. 88.

But God, who is rich in mercy, out of the great love with which he loved us even when we were dead through our trespasses, made us alive together with Christ-- by grace you have been saved-- and raised us up with him and seated us with him in the heavenly places in Christ Jesus, so that in the ages to come he might show the immeasurable riches of his grace in kindness toward us in Christ Jesus. For by grace you have been saved through faith, and this is not your own doing; it is the gift of God.
-Ephesians 2:4-8 NRSV-

Anyone who had ever filled a birdfeeder knows how quickly birds can clean it out. Often times, like Wendell Berry describes, more is wasted than eaten, and seed is not cheap. By reflecting on the imagery offered by Berry it is easy to see parallels between the feeding of the wasteful birds and the gospel message.

We, like the birds, did not deserve the first gift. The man sets out seed because he loves the birds and wants to share in their lives. God gave us life, and the freedom to respond to his love with love of our own. Yet like the birds we freely squander the gift; taking without acknowledgment of its source; wasting more than we take. Yet, unlike the birds, our waste ran deeper. We turned our God-given freedom into rebellion against him. Our rebellion left us, as the passage in Ephesians says, "dead through our trespasses." God had every right to walk away and leave us in our condition. He knew the cost of bringing us back to life. He bought the seed, to make it free.

When I read that line in the poem, and read the Ephesian's passage in connection with the narrative of Passion Week, I cannot help but think of the cost. God should have left us in our state of death, cut off from the source of life that we rebelled from. But God, who is rich in mercy, out of the depths of his great love, made us alive in Christ. The cost for our life was his. And through his self-sacrificial death, he made life possible. Through the Father raising the Son from the dead, he made it actual. "By faith you have been saved through faith."

All that is required of the birds is that they "take and eat" freely from the bounty set before them. All that is required of us, it to "take and eat" from the richness of God's grace that he has set before us. Because God has "bought the seed, to make it free." This exquisite gift that cost so much, is freely given.

Discussion Questions:

Some many of us have heard the Gospel message so many times that it loses its power.

❖ How do we hear this message with fresh ears?

❖ How can we reimagine the sacrifice of Christ so others can hear the Good News?

❖ Do we need to repent of wasting the gift God has freely given?

Prayer:

> We pray, oh God, for your patience with us to continue. We pray that we can recognize the gift you have given, and order our lives accordingly. We pray for those who have never heard the story our gift. Let our lives be a sign that you have made us alive again.
>
> Glory be to the Father, and to the Son, and to the Holy
> > Spirit.
> As it was in the beginning, is now and ever shall ever be,
> > world without end.
> Alleluia.
> Amen.

DAY THIRTY-EIGHT: ABIDE IN ME

"It's not death that makes the dead rise out of the ground, but something alive straining up, rooted in darkness, like a vine."
New Collected Poems, "The Birth [Near Port William]," 146.

I am the true vine, and my Father is the vinegrower. He removes every branch in me that bears no fruit. Every branch that bears fruit he prunes to make it bear more fruit. You have already been cleansed by the word that I have spoken to you. Abide in me as I abide in you. Just as the branch cannot bear fruit by itself unless it abides in the vine, neither can you unless you abide in me. I am the vine, you are the branches. Those who abide in me and I in them bear much fruit, because apart from me you can do nothing.
-John 15:1-5 NRSV-

Jesus speaks these words to his disciples during his last meal with them. Judas has just been dismissed to fulfill his betrayal of Jesus, and the eleven remain while Jesus gives a long discourse of last-minute thoughts and blessings. Jesus says to them, "Abide in me." I am not entirely sure that the Disciples know what is coming in the days ahead. I am not even sure they know that it is their last meal with Jesus. Things are about to get really rough, and they don't know it yet.

Jesus' words are pastoral instructions for them. When things are going well and it seems like just another day with your friends, abide in me. When you leave this place, after spending sacred moments together and allowing me to wash your feet, and go forth to deny me not once but three times, abide in me. When your Rabbi is taken before the high priest and Pilate and accused of many things, abide in me. When I am mocked, teased, beaten beyond recognition, and crowned with thorns, abide in me. When you watch the one you have been following these past few years, the one who changed your entire life by calling you to follow, carry a cross alone to his own crucifixion, abide in me.

As you gaze upon your savior, dying on a cruel cross before an even crueler crowd and you have no idea why, abide in me. When your closest friends, with whom you have shared life and without whom you know not how to function, scatter and you are left to figure things out alone, abide in me.

Jesus' words to them are for us as well. When all is well, abide in me. When you deny your Lord by your actions or your lack thereof, abide in me. When you no longer know who I am because life has conflicted everything you thought you knew about me, abide in me. When your lack of knowing who I am gets worse because those who bear my name do bad things to you or others in the name of religion, abide in me. When suffering comes not knocking but tearing down your door, abide in me. When all seems lost and your last ray of hope slips beyond the clouds, abide in me. When those who know you best and who once could help you make sense of the chaos of life can no longer reach your desperate place, abide in me.

Resurrection could only come on the other side of a cross. Jesus could not taste resurrection without tasting suffering and death. How then could we expect to be greater than our Master? The message of the cross is that our Lord suffers with us, deep in the depths of our being, where no one else can go. Only from those depths can the beauty of Resurrection come. Only from those depths can come "something alive straining up," that lets us know that we are truly alive.

Discussion Questions:

❖ Is it possible to believe that true life can come out of deep darkness?

❖ How have you seen the power of Resurrection in your life?

Prayer:

God of Day and God of Darkness, thank you that when I experience darkness in the depths of my being, you can bring forth life. Thank you for the power of Resurrection. Help me to trust that power even today. Amen.

DAY THIRTY-NINE: THE SILENCE OF GOD

"Outside the window
is a roofed wooden tray
he fills with seeds for the birds. . .
At first they came fearfully, worried
by the man's movements
inside the room. They watched
his eyes, and flew
when he looked. Now they expect
no harm from him
and forget he's there.
they come into his vision,
unafraid. He keeps
a certain distance and quietness
in tribute to them.
That they ignore him
he takes in tribute to himself."
    New Collected Poems, "Window Poems," 8. 88.

The word of the LORD was rare in those days; visions were not widespread.

                                            -1 Samuel 3:1 NRS-

This verse from 1 Samuel is striking in how contemporary it sounds. As we try and think of how many people we know that have received visions or a word from the Lord, we are left with the stark realization that they are rare in our days. I have had discussions with people who even doubt the existence of God because they see so little evidence of the miraculous hand of God that is witnessed to in the Bible. Yet even here the Bible testifies to the silence of God.

Wendell Berry's imagery of the man and the birds gives an excellent picture of this silence. When the birds see the man they are fearful, so the man keeps his distance and hides his movements to allow the birds the freedom to accept his gift. He even takes a measure of pride in his the fact that they no longer notice him, because he allows them the freedom to dine unafraid. God likewise can seem distant, and his movements remain unseen or unnoticed. It does not mean that he is not there nor does it mean that he is angry. Perhaps, God's aloofness is part of his gift of freedom. He has given us the gift of life, but if he were to overshadow us with his majesty, we would unable to exercise his gift.

However, both the feeder of the birds and the Giver of life are fully present the whole time. Simple because we do not perceive God does not mean that he is not present. Particularly in times of great need, we witness God move in powerful ways. In the narrative following this verse the corruption of the priests in Israel led God to raise up Samuel as a prophet who would anoint kings of Israel. God reveals his closeness when we need him most. Maybe this is what Paul meant in 2 Corinthians 12:9 when he said that God's power is made perfect in weakness. God may be silent, but be assured that he is close by watching you use the free life he gave you. Spend it wisely.

Discussion Questions:
- ❖ The silence of God can be deafening:
- ❖ Have you ever experience a period where God seemed silent or distant? Explain.
- ❖ How did this period affect you spiritual life?
- ❖ How can you be mindful of the presence of Christ when it feels like you are all alone? How can you help others as they experience the same?

Prayer:

> We pray, oh God, that your silence does not last past our endurance. We ask for your word to reach our hardened hearts. We pray for visions to shake our comfortable lives and remind us of our purpose. We ask that when your silence does envelop us, that we never forget you, and order our lives around your Truth.

> Glory be to the Father, and to the Son, and to the Holy
>> Spirit.
> As it was in the beginning, is now and ever shall ever be,
>> world without end.
> Alleluia.
> Amen.

DAY FORTY: THE BODY AND THE RESURRECTION

"What death means is not this – the spirit, triumphant in the body's fall, praising its absence, feeding on music. If life can't justify and explain itself, death can't justify and explain it."
New Collected Poems, "Canticle," 19.

For we know that if the earthly tent we live in is destroyed, we have a building from God, a house not made with hands, eternal in the heavens. For in this tent we groan, longing to be clothed with our heavenly dwelling – if indeed, when we have taken it off we will not be found naked. For while we are still in this tent, we groan under our burden, because we wish not to be unclothed but to be further clothed, so that what is mortal may be swallowed up by life.

-2 Corinthians 5:1-4 NRSV-

I was once at a Christian conference where a small group leader said that it does not matter how we treat creation now, because God is a God of restoration, and God will make all things new. He included that in order to be made new, creation as we know it must first be destroyed.

Sadly, I think his view is fairly common. What is the point of taking care of the earth if it will one day be destroyed anyway? More specifically, what is the point of taking care of our bodies if they will be destroyed?

What if he is wrong? What if God is not interested at all in destroying the works of God's hands, but rather in restoring it by giving it new life? Paul writes that our bodies are longing for our heavenly home, the home where we truly belong, in the place where all things are restored to wholeness.

When Jesus was resurrected three days after his death, he made certain to appear in bodily form to his disciples. Thomas touched his hands and side. Jesus ate fish by the sea. He walked with Peter and instructed him to feed his sheep. Bodily resurrection was a very important part of Jesus' ministry.

Berry writes that death is not the soul rejoicing without the body. For Berry, as with Jesus, bodily resurrection is a very important part of our faith. Maybe Jesus is not only concerned with the healing and restoration of our souls, but of our bodies as well. Surely, then, as we work toward bringing God's Kingdom into reality on earth, or in other words making life on earth as it is in heaven, that also includes taking care of the bodies that will one day be resurrected and united fully with our spirits.

Discussion Questions:

- ❖ Does how we treat our bodies now have any impact on eternity?
- ❖ Can the soul be well without the wellness of the body? Are the two intertwined?

Prayer:

God, you have created us with both a body and a soul. Thank you that you care for both. As we seek to be more like you, help us to care for both our bodies and our souls as equally created and loved by you. Amen.

Bibliography:

Berry, Wendell. *New Collected Poems*. Berkeley: Counterpoint, 2012.

Berry, Wendell. *That Distant Land*. Berkeley: Counterpoint, 2004.

Berry, Wendell. *The Art of the Commonplace: The Agrarian Essays of Wendell Berry.* Berkeley: Counterpoint, 2003.

Bosch, David J. *Transforming Mission: Paradigm Shifts in Theology of Mission.* Maryknoll: Orbis, 1991.

National Center for Education Statistics. "Number and Percentage of Public School Students Eligible for Free or Reduced-Price Lunch, by State: Selected Years, 2000-01 through 2011-12." *Digest of Education Statistics,* Table 204.10. Cited 14 April 2015. Online: https://nces.ed.gov/programs/digest/d13/tables/dt13_204.10.asp.

World Food Programme. "Hunger Statistics." No Pages. Cited 14 April 2015. Online: http://www.wfp.org/hunger/stats.

Wiederkehr, Macrina. *Seven Sacred Pauses*. Notre Dame: Sorin Books, 2008.

Made in the USA
Middletown, DE
23 February 2023